THE TAO OF THE
LOVING COUPLE

THE TAO OF THE LOVING COUPLE

True Liberation through the Tao

JOLAN CHANG

E. P. DUTTON □ NEW YORK

First published 1983

Copyright © 1983 by Jolan Chang
All rights reserved. Printed in the U.S.A.

Published in the United States by
E. P. Dutton,
a division of NAL Penguin Inc.,
2 Park Avenue, New York, N.Y. 10016.

Library of Congress Catalog Card Number: 83-71316

ISBN: 0-525-48042-0 (paper)

Published simultaneously in Canada by
Fitzhenry & Whiteside Limited, Toronto

Designed by Nancy Etheredge

10 9 8 7 6 5

To all those
who are contributing
toward saving our world
from being destroyed.

CONTENTS

PREFACE

Several years have passed since the publication of my first book, *The Tao of Love and Sex.* Though the book was written mainly to help men, more than 80 percent of the letters I received were from women. Because of this encouragement, the idea of writing a book of Tao for *both partners* gradually took root.

I have observed over and over that with sufficient love people become healthier and more efficient in every respect. For a woman, in particular, love can carry over to becoming a tender, more loving mother, a fact that will have an incalculable consequence on future generations. And I have learned by experience that the most effective way to secure sufficient love for both men and women is to show women how to influence men gently to become more adequate lovers.

I am convinced that the Tao as a philosophy can help women achieve true liberation without bitter and costly confrontations. Only by uniting the two sexes in equality, love, and harmony can we expect to save the world from catastrophe. With such loving collaboration we may even manage to create a better world.

I have written this book to accomplish the above-mentioned purposes. It is also a kind of open letter answering the questions asked by readers of my first book, as well as an expression of my appreciation and gratitude to readers for their boundless enthusiasm.

This book is more than a sex manual. The Tao, the oldest philosophy of life, gives the simplest answer: *Life is living, and our task is to live wholesomely, happily, and freely.* That is what this book is all about.

Jolan Chang

ACKNOWLEDGMENTS

The author would like to give special thanks to Joseph Needham F.R.S., F.B.A., lately Master of Gonville and Caius College, Cambridge, and author of the monumental series "Science and Civilization in China," and to Dr. Eric Trimmer, editor of the British *Journal of Sexual Medicine*, for their encouragement and advice; to Ina Svensson, who typed the manuscript more than twice; to all friends who provided the necessary inspiration; and last but certainly not least to Dutton's Senior Editor Bill Whitehead for his infinite patience and valuable suggestions.

THE TAO OF THE LOVING COUPLE

1. THE TAO OF LOVING AND HAPPINESS

What is it men in women do require?
The lineaments of Gratified Desire.
What is it women in men do require?
The lineaments of Gratified Desire.

WILLIAM BLAKE
THE QUESTION ANSWERED

Love, unlike money, can bring happiness.

I have no secret to tell you about how to become rich because I do not know how. After reading stories about heiresses like Barbara Hutton and billionaires like Getty, Hughes, and Onassis, I am very much convinced that they were not very happy people. As Barbara Hutton said herself shortly before her death: "You cannot buy love. . . . My money has never brought me happiness."*

What I can and am going to tell you is how to be a happy lover and therefore become a happy person.

---

*Quoted by Enid Nemy in *The Observer*, May 13, 1979.

1

THE CURSE OF IMPOTENCE

When I was about thirty and living in Toronto, Canada, I was for a period almost helplessly impotent—a problem nearly all men face at some time in their lives.

To be impotent is to be in a most awkward situation. In his arms he holds a woman who fully desires him and expects him to love her, but he cannot. In my case, the impotence was the unhappy result of twelve years of ejaculation almost every day, often more than just once. Erroneously, a therapist at the University of California speaks of people "who have had so much sex in the last ten or fifteen years that the thrill has declined."* It is not sex or love that kills the thrill or causes impotence; it is unrestrained, uncontrolled ejaculation.

Since my brief, unhappy experience with impotence, I have been making love for more than thirty years at least three or four times more frequently than I did in those early twelve years. The result? *Love-making has not lost any of its thrill for me. In fact, I like it today much more than ever before.*

HOW A WOMAN HELPED ME CONQUER IMPOTENCE

The woman I liked very much at that time was a very unusual person. Even though I was not able to make love often because of my periodic impotence, she had great patience. Besides, she was always ready. As Li Tung Hsüan says: "Her coral cave is inundated and overflowing, as a silent spring descending a deep valley."† Under such a favorable condition, I thought, it would not be too difficult to enter her by manipulation, even with a flaccid phallus.

So I used my fingers to launch my half-erect penis into her flooded vulva, and with beginner's luck I succeeded the very first time. Through the years, with practice, I have become so proficient that I am now able to push in even a totally limp penis.

To my surprise, I found that when I became expert in manipulating my penis my confidence in myself as a man automatically and propor-

*Klaus Mehnert, *Twilight of the Young* (New York: Holt, Rinehart and Winston, 1976), p. 243.
†Li Tung Hsüan, *Tung Hsüan Tzu*, chapter 5, a seventh-century book of the Tao.

tionately increased. As a result, the problem of impotence vanished. We know that impotence is mainly a problem of fear and lack of confidence, but the cure for it using one's own fingers is not quite so well known. More than thirty years ago I named the technique "soft entry."

When soft entry is combined with ejaculation control, as advised in the ancient Tao, a man is almost unbeatable! I thought I had discovered something entirely new—something revolutionary and original. Many years later, however, I found the equivalent of soft entry in a reprint of a 2,000-year-old text by Wu Hsien.* Those ancient Taoists knew a thing or two!

Mind you, an ancient Chinese text is not at all easy to decipher. And the Tao of Loving has not been properly studied since the late Ming Dynasty, in the last part of the sixteenth century. After repeated reading into Wu Hsien's text, I found four Chinese characters that caught my eye: *Tho Zer Chan Zoo. Tho* means "soft, weak, limp"; *Zer* means "in, to enter"; *Chan* means "strong, stiff"; *Zoo* means "to withdraw, to leave." Together they could be translated into two phrases: "Weak in, stiff withdraw." They looked very puzzling. If I had not stumbled upon soft entry myself earlier, I would not have understood what they meant. In reality, these two phrases represent the two essential principles of the Tao of Loving. Mastering the first, a couple can make love at almost any time and as frequently as their hearts desire. Mastering the second, a young man can control his ejaculation and at the same time make himself an almost completely safe lover; his woman will never again have to use contraceptives when she makes love with him. (I use the word *almost* here only because nothing on earth is truly 100 percent safe.)

I have used the withdrawal method exclusively with or without the Tao's ejaculation control† for more than forty years without a single accident.

When I conquered my impotence, my life was changed completely for the better. I have become a very happy person and lover. I hope to convince you that the Tao can help almost any person achieve loving bliss.

---

*Wu Hsien, *Shu Chin Yu Lu,* chapter 18.
†Jolan Chang, *The Tao of Love and Sex* (New York: E. P. Dutton, 1977), chapter 3.

AVA

Ava is not her true name, but she is a real person who has agreed to let me write about her. Her family background is not at all happy. Her father is an alcoholic, as is her grandmother and her grandmother's man friend. Her mother is a beautiful, angelic woman with extremely soft skin. A nonsmoker and nondrinker (so is Ava), she divorced her husband more than fifteen years ago.

Ava is one of the most loving, straightforward people I have ever met. Without hesitation she told me her personal stories, one by one. I learned almost immediately that she had three lovers and she did not hesitate to have me as the fourth.

Ava is only twenty-four, already a promising artist. She does not pay much attention to her clothing, so you may not think her attractive if you meet her on the street. But when her unbecoming clothing is removed, an extremely beautiful woman emerges. Her soft, smooth, jade-like skin (an inheritance from her mother, she says) and her magnificent figure make her a most exquisite person to behold and to hold. My spontaneous impression was that she resembled Botticelli's goddess in "The Birth of Venus."

I should mention here the difference between the concept of beauty as expressed in the Tao and the more common yardsticks. According to the ancient Tao text, the most outstanding woman is one who is warm, sympathetic, and harmonious—as opposed to a hard, cold, and artificially beautiful woman whose attractiveness cannot endure a long association.

Ava is also one of the warmest, most affectionate women I have ever met. She loves to make love. At our second meeting, on a Friday evening, she brought some of her drawings to show me. They were surprisingly good for one so young. Soon after her arrival we began to love each other most naturally—she is one of the few women I have ever met who has the charm and fascination of total freedom. There is no vestige of inhibition in her. And I have hardly ever met a woman whose body could be so totally fused with mine. We made love most of the night and much of the next morning. What happened the next time was even more memorable. She arrived about 10:00 P.M., after her foreign language class. It was a cold, snowy night, so she took a hot bath immediately after coming in. She began to tell me of her previous evening with her Brazilian lover. (She would always tell me all her loving activities in detail, and I noticed that each time after meeting with other lovers she would love me more affectionately.)

A moment later she explained, "Jolan, when I make love with you I feel like we are playing a duet of classic composition and dancing a classic pas de deux. With José I feel like we are playing the music of the Amazon and dancing a jungle Indian dance."

Making love once was never quite enough for Ava. In her own words: "The more and longer, the better I like it." And one could see that she was telling the truth. Because the longer we made love, the more her face would light up in an angelic glow. With each successive love-making, the expression on her face became more ecstatic. It was the look of a truly happy and satisfied woman.

We have been happy together every time, but that night and morning we were so extremely happy that we called ourselves "the glorious lovers." We made love at least five times before we fell asleep and four or five times more before we got up, around a quarter to eight. It makes me shudder to remember what David Reuben said: "The third copulation of the evening is more for the record books than the enjoyment of the participants."*

ON ATTRACTIVENESS

What makes such a beautiful young woman love a man her grandfather's age? First, I do not look my age. Very few people would take me for more than forty, and some think me as young as thirty. Lawrence Durrell, the famed novelist, thought I looked eighteen when I stepped down from the train to meet him for the first time several years ago. Our long weekend together so inspired him that he wrote a little book mainly about the Tao and me, *A Smile in the Mind's Eye.* The following is his description:

> As he stepped down from the ladder I took him to be about eighteen, so supple and light were his movements. He smiled and waved and then leaped to the *quai* as lightly as a cat. Yes, it was Chang all right! It was a lit-

*David Reuben, *Everything You Always Wanted to Know About Sex* (New York: Avon Books, 1971).

6

tle while before I found out that this slim Chinese youth was around sixty years of age!*

Youthful looks, however, cannot be the only reason for my success with Ava. A loving and affectionate woman, fond of making love, will usually find a man who practices the Tao extremely attractive—for the simple reason that the Tao provides him with an ability to satisfy her thoroughly. Through the years I have noticed many times that women tend to truly love men who completely satisfy their loving needs. And my observation and experiences bear out what Blake says:

> *What is it women do in men require?*
> *The lineaments of Gratified Desire.*

This is of course true for men as well. Many a man would give up almost everything else to be with a woman who truly makes him happy.

Can everybody follow this path, regardless of age and sex? Just read on and you will discover that the Tao is actually quite easy to learn if you believe in it. And it will change your life completely for the better!

I know an Australian woman, in her fifties, neither wealthy nor famous, who manages to live a happy and fulfilled life by advising younger and less experienced women and men how to love. Without benefit of the Tao, she has arrived at some similar conclusions by her own observations and experience. Here is part of a letter she wrote to a young protégé of hers about how a woman may teach men to become happier lovers:

> The woman teaches the man the postponement of what he wants through erotic play. You need sensitive men for that. The first step is to get men used to holding hands while you talk about casual or deep things; to have physical closeness, hands, arms pressed close while the mind is occupied with something else—say, talking about his childhood. . . . Otherwise, the moment the male touches the female he wants *sex*. This is especially true in the English-speaking world, where touching between people is taboo even in childhood. *There is no other way of uniting people but through bodily union.*

*Lawrence Durrell, *A Smile in the Mind's Eye* (New York: Universe Books, 1982), p. 3.

You encourage the person with whom you are becoming close through nonsexual sex, saying how wonderful it is, *how peace streams into you by touching him*, and so on. Gradually, the male will become conscious of this touching. Teach each little bit of skin and muscle joy through touching, stroking. Do this with hands and lips. Gradually extend this to arms, neck, back, and front.

2. SOME TRIUMPHS OF THE TAO

During 23 days in every month (in the absence of pregnancy) from the time a woman is 7 years old till she dies of old age, she is ready for action and competent. As competent as the candlestick is to receive the candle. Competent every day, competent every night. Also, she wants that candle—yearns for it, longs for it, hankers after it....

MARK TWAIN

In his posthumously published *Letters from the Earth*, Mark Twain humorously describes the amazing vitality of feminine sexuality.* He goes on to portray the relatively minute capacity of the average man, which according to his estimate is only about 3 percent of his female counterpart.

Allowing for certain exaggeration for dramatic purposes, Twain's observation is extremely astute, one that concurs with both the findings of the ancient Tao and those of modern research, especially the Sherfey theory.†

---

*Mark Twain, *Letters from the Earth* (New York: Harper & Row, 1962), p. 40.
†Mary Jane Sherfey, as cited in Norman Mailer, *The Prisoner of Sex* (New York: Signet, 1971), pp. 56–57. The Sherfey theory is summarized briefly in the last chapter of this book.

10

Are the sexes, then, hopelessly mismatched? Do not despair. The Tao can help to change this state of affairs.

MY WIFE WANTS THREE COPULATIONS DAILY

A reader of my first book wrote to me to express his concern when he heard about a man who was hard-pressed by his wife's desire for three sessions of love-making daily. The husband wrote to a local doctor for advice. As could be expected, the doctor advised restrained compromise. But could such advice really help to save the marriage? The husband had already done his utmost, so the wife was the one who had to exercise all the restraint and compromise her robust sexuality.

My reader wrote me because he felt that only the Tao offers an effective means of equalizing the imbalance in sexual capacity in most man–woman relationships. The following is an example of how the Tao helped to save a marriage in a similar situation.

A HUSBAND IN DESPAIR

> Kazantzakis, the famous Greek writer, regarded a young man in his twenties as one of the great philosophers of Spain. This young man believed that all the problems of the world might be solved if only one could solve the problem that has always existed between man and woman. Unfortunately, this philosopher died when he was thirty. He drowned himself. Over a woman.*

Shortly after giving a talk to the Society for Oriental Studies at the University of Upsala (forty miles north of Stockholm), I received a phone call from a young man who had attended my talk. His voice was full of alarm. He wanted to bring his wife to visit me as soon as possible. They came the next afternoon. They were both under thirty years old, with two young children. They were obviously very tender and devoted to each other.

Almost as soon as they began to tell me their problem, they started to weep. Several months earlier the wife had met another young man, and all her bottled physical passion was awakened by this new encounter.

*Alexander Wolf, "The Problem of Infidelity," in Salo Rosenbaum and Jan Alger, eds., *The Marriage Relationship* (New York: Basic Books, 1968).

Theirs was a very honest marriage, and the wife told the husband what had happened.

By one look I could see that there was a great physical disparity between the couple: The husband was affectionate but physically far from strong; the wife, a model of wholesomeness, had a voluptuous body. And the man had, not surprisingly, begun to worry about losing her. Instead of doing something positive, he had started to smoke and drink large quantities of alcohol and black coffee. The unsurprising result was that he had begun to suffer from insomnia and had started to lose weight. He became an even less effective partner for a healthy and passionate woman. The couple seemed to have reached an impasse.

My immediate advice was to pull the husband out from his self-destructive course. He should immediately strengthen his body by reducing his daily intake of cigarettes, alcohol, and coffee to the bare minimum. And he should start eating large quantities of wheat germ, with milk. I advised them to sleep very close together, preferably holding or at least touching each other. I told them not to be concerned about actual love-making at this stage. They were to ring me again in one month.

The wife telephoned a month later to inform me that their life had greatly improved. She asked if she could come to visit me alone, as there were things she could not easily tell me with her husband present. She came the next day and told me in detail what happened when she met the other young man, who was a much better lover. For the first time she realized the true capacity of her own passion and how much she needed physical love.

I gave her a few instructions so that she might make her husband an equally good lover or even a better one. The secret of my instructions was to depart from the usual orgasm-oriented way of loving and to sharpen their senses so that they would be able to enjoy love-making much more frequently. Specifically, my advice was this:

1. Whenever possible, especially on the weekends, the couple should stay in bed—not to sleep but to caress and cuddle each other.

2. Whenever the wife wanted him to enter her, the husband should apply the "soft entry" technique. (I have described this briefly in Chapter 1; for more detail, see Chapter 8 of my first book, *The Tao of Love and Sex*.) He should enter her softly, in every sense of the word.

3. The husband should help with his fingers and try to thrust gently, as described in Chapter 1.

4. He should stop thrusting immediately whenever he felt that he had to ejaculate.

5. They should apply vegetable oil either on his penis or on her vulva or both. In their case the oil was not really necessary, for she was very wet nearly all the time. In fact, she even went to see a doctor for that. Fortunately, the doctor was a good one and advised her that it was just a sign of being healthy.*

In this case the wife was a very warm and astute woman and she understood everything I said, at least intuitively. She promised to telephone me as soon as they succeeded in carrying out my instructions.

And within five days she called: "It's wonderful! We have made it. Yesterday my sister looked after our children for us, and since it was Sunday we were able to stay in bed almost all day long and make love as you prescribed. My husband was not even tired at all!"

JULIE'S PROBLEM

Julie is very beautiful but she looks much older than her twenty-five years. Ever since she was fifteen she has not been able to find a man who could gratify her desire. And Julie's desire seems to confirm Mark Twain's observation, quoted earlier. Unfortunately, each time she would find a man, he would invariably take flight. Her healthy, uninhibited appetite for loving frightened each of her potential lovers. Added to her problem was her dislike of masturbation.

---

*Unfortunately, not all doctors are like this one and some even prescribe medicine to dry up the female parts. Such advice could be a horrible mistake. I always tell women who worry unnecessarily about easily becoming wet that they should consider themselves lucky. There are two exceptions, of course—when the secretion has an unpleasant smell or when there is irritation.

I once had a rather lengthy talk with a reader of my first book about applying vegetable oil. She said that a foreign lubricant like oil should never be used. I advised that when it came to a subject like that it is always better to be flexible. And vegetable oil is cheap, harmless, and wholesome. Our body tissues can easily absorb it without any adverse effect. I regard it as a savior of many unnecessary irritations and inconveniences.

To Julie, the pain of love hunger was infinitely more excruciating than hunger for food. For many years she felt that life was not worth living because of that hunger. Often she thought of killing herself by cutting her wrists. Instead she chose the easier and slower path to self-destruction—heavy smoking and drinking. For more than a year and a half she got drunk about five out of every seven days. She was on her way to becoming an alcoholic.

Luckily, Julie had a strong instinct for life. One day she realized she had to snap out of it or she would become an alcoholic. She cut down her drinking greatly. She also went through a three-year period of psychotherapy, which helped her to feel a little less lonely, a little less desperate. She continued, however, to smoke heavily, still got drunk about two times a week, and cried inconsolably just about every night.

Reading the Swedish version of *The Tao of Love and Sex* was a breakthrough for Julie. She bought two more copies and posted them to two of her male friends who had been her lovers but had been frightened away by her healthy appetite. Happily, one of them responded favorably. About four months later Julie telephoned to tell me the good news: "I want you to know that your book has practically given me a new life." I met her and her lover a few days later and they told me a heartening story.

Julie's healthy appetite for loving, though it scared men away, was in reality only natural. According to the Tao, this is a manifestation of woman's inborn urge for the harmony of Yin and Yang. A man who knows the Tao would welcome such a woman with open arms. Unfortunately, few men today know how this can and should be done.

Before reading the Tao, Julie and her lover Thomas, like most people, measured man–woman satisfaction in terms of orgasms and ejaculations. When a relationship is based on such a dubious foundation, it is hard to achieve true satisfaction. As a rule, neither of the partners arrives at the exalted state of true harmony by the conventional man-must-ejaculate route. For, when a man makes love in the conventional way, he usually finds his partner unsatisfied, still craving for more loving after his ejaculation. But he himself is definitely finished, at least for the time being. Of course, some women will pretend to be satisfied each time to please the man, but that never solves the problem. It only builds up tension and resentment and leads to an eventual explosion.

15

No sensitive man can really be satisfied in love-making when his partner is not. Because of that, the man usually finds himself in a most delicate and difficult position after ejaculation. He wants to help but he cannot. He is not unlike a soldier in heavy fighting who suddenly realizes that he has used up all his ammunition.

In such an awkward situation a conventional sexologist would advise afterplay, which mainly implies digital stimulation. Of course, many men have tried that, many more are still trying it, and some may be doing it every time. Such stimulation poses at least three problems. First, it is not all that easy to use one's fingers to satisfy a woman. It can be as difficult and as delicate as playing a musical instrument. Second, many women do not like their clitorises and vulvas manipulated by fingers. Third, too much digital stimulation can be tiresome for both partners, and no ideal relationship can be maintained in this manner for very long. Some sexologists comfort their clients by saying that fingers can be even better than sexual organs. This may be true, but only if one has not learned how to use one's sexual organs properly!

Julie and Thomas discovered after experimenting with the Tao that the secret of loving is not only learning how to use one's sexual organs properly. The true happiness of loving depends mainly in a successful fusion of two bodies into one—the harmony of Yin and Yang.

Before the Tao, Julie believed that loving satisfaction for a woman depended on orgasms. The more numerous and more intense the orgasms, the more the woman would be satisfied.

Things began to change dramatically as soon as they started testing the Tao. First of all, Julie noticed that Thomas could make love to her almost daily, often many times daily. Then she noticed that she was not quite so desperately hungry as she had been before. With her hunger reduced, she did not reach orgasm each time she made love. She discovered that the hungrier she was, the quicker, more numerous, and more intense her orgasms would be. In fact, when she was really hungry, she could easily reach an orgasm or even a chain of orgasms just by placing her lover's leg tightly against her vulva.

Finally she realized that loving satisfaction could not be directly identified with orgasm. What she now believes is that it is nice to have orgasms sometimes, but the most important, most satisfying pleasure is the fusion of two bodies as often as possible. She needs at least one love-making session every two days (with the Tao a session usually includes several rounds of love-making). If she has only two sessions a week she feels quite hungry. Six or seven days without love-making used to make Julie desperate; it was then that she would feel the urge to smoke heavily to dull her senses, and to get drunk to escape the pain. For the first time in her life, Julie now feels the joy of living.

Julie's love partner, Thomas, also discovered something new and interesting. Like most other men, before the Tao he had always regarded ejaculation and male orgasm (a subject to be discussed in the next chapter) as one and the same. Now he no longer believes that. Before the Tao, each love-making session was like waging battle, and he was tense and nervous before each encounter. And with Julie he could never win. Even though he often succeeded in waiting for Julie's orgasm before his own ejaculation, he was out of luck, because Julie's one orgasm was not enough if she had not made love for five days or more. But Thomas was thirty-seven years old, and for him repeated love-making in the conventional way (ejaculation each time) was very exhausting. After meeting Julie more than once a week for about seven weeks, he could no longer go on. No matter how much he liked her, he had to bow out. They remained friendly, but he avoided making love with her.

After reading the copy of my book that Julie had sent him, Thomas reacted quickly. He telephoned her to say he would be interested in giving it a try.

What did Thomas find out? After just a few tries he found it not at all difficult to love according to the Tao. In fact, even before reading the Tao he had often felt he did not really want to ejaculate each time he made love. At these times he would force his ejaculation, because he had been indoctrinated with the conventional myth that a man must ejaculate each time. The Tao gave him the support he needed to break away from that nonsense!

Without ejaculation each time, Thomas found he was no longer so nervous about making love, and afterward he was less exhausted. Now he can make love almost any time Julie wants. He no longer feels annoyed or frightened when Julie expresses her desire for more. On the contrary, the more she wants, the more he likes it. In other words, he had never felt so good before about love and life.

Like Julie he has also discovered that total contact, a fusion of two

bodies and souls, the harmony of Yin and Yang, is the greatest joy in life. In comparison with this great joy, the spasmodic sensation of ejaculation is nothing.

Says Julie: "I am not exaggerating at all to say that the Tao has saved my life. Before the Tao, for many years I lived a wretched life that was not a life at all. I was constantly tortured from a desperate hunger for love. The pain of that hunger was so excruciating that I felt there was no point in living. Consequently I was always seeking self-destruction, consciously or unconsciously.

"The Tao has changed all that. I still feel hungry sometimes—in fact, quite often—but it is a healthy hunger without the pain and fear of starvation. What a sense of security this gives me!

"The Tao has not only given me constant satisfaction. It has made love-making and life ecstatically beautiful. Before the Tao, though I sometimes had satisfaction in making love, it was always something so momentary, so devastatingly uncertain! There was never enough time and opportunity to taste and feel the exquisiteness of love-making. Now I can really feel that Thomas is with me, in me, and so often. Our love-making before the Tao can only be called 'sex.' Now I can truly call it 'love.' And I love Thomas so dearly now, a feeling I never had with anyone before. Truly, I feel that loving in the way of Tao is by far the most beautiful thing in this world!"

And Thomas: "The Tao has made me a man at last and a very happy man at that. Before, I was just an unhappy coward constantly running away from women. The more loving, affectionate, and beautiful a woman was, the more I was afraid. I am not at all afraid of women anymore, thanks to the Tao and to Julie. Now I feel I truly love Julie. Making love to her is the most wonderful thing in the world. But without the Tao this could never have been possible. Before the Tao, as soon as she reached an explosive orgasm,* or more often even long before that, I lost control and was finished. Then when I looked at her pleading eyes and desire for more, I felt so helpless that I wished I could disappear. What else could I do?

---

*The conventional wisdom holds that a woman's orgasm and a man's ejaculation should occur at approximately the same time. But when a woman needs repeated love-making this certainly is not ideal. And according to the Tao, most women need repeated love-making.

When I had my ejaculation, I could lose my wish for making love for a whole week!

"But this has been changed completely. From the Tao I have learned how to control the situation. No matter how explosively Julie reaches her orgasms, I keep control of the situation and it gives me a confidence, a satisfaction, that is worth hundreds of ejaculations. In fact, it cannot really be compared. When you see and feel that your love partner is ecstatically happy and know that you are greatly contributing to this happiness, you experience the most wonderful feeling in the world.

"What is more, now that I have learned ejaculation control, I ejaculate only when I really feel the need. The result is that now even after an ejaculation I can make love again in about twenty minutes. Before, I often forced ejaculation, and it could take me days to recover."

3. THE ORGASMIC CONFUSION

THE TAO AND ORGASMIC ANXIETY

Where does pathology begin?

Where does normality end?

What constitutes a true orgasmic inhibition?

What should be considered a normal variation of the female sexual response?

When is treatment indicated?

When should the woman be reassured that she is normal?

Again, at this time the answers to these crucial questions are speculative and highly controversial.

At one end of the spectrum of opinion is the psychoanalytic view, which posits that any woman who does not have orgasm during intercourse is neurotic and frigid, even if she enjoys sex. . . .

At the other end of the spectrum are some feminists who regard clitoral orgasm as the norm, and consider orgasm experienced during coitus a manifestation of female submission to the male. . . . *

*Helen Singer Kaplan, The New Sex Therapy (New York: Brunner-Mazel, 1974), pp. 380–381.

21

Listening to this thoughtful lament from an eminent physician-therapist like Helen Kaplan, one feels that the Tao's wisdom on the subject is infinitely superior. The term *orgasm* does not appear in the Tao. Its terms are *enjoyment* and *satisfaction*. When we make love we must learn and do our best to feel and enjoy it. If we do not feel satisfied the first time, we should try again and again until we are satiated. (This of course implies that men first learn the Tao's way of loving so that they are able to try again and again.)

This method would make unnecessary the eternal, pointless argument whether women have two different kinds of orgasms, vaginal and clitoral. All experienced sexologists know that orgasms vary from woman to woman: Some women have an orgasm as if being struck by a thunderbolt or experiencing a fainting spell. At the other extreme are women who have an orgasm as indifferent as a hiccup or a yawn! In between, there are hundreds of variations.

Also, there are many different ways for women to reach orgasm. A few of them may achieve it by just embracing and kissing a man. Or a woman may require both her own and her lover's infinite patience to attain orgasm through concentrated digital manipulation of her clitoris for half an hour or more. Some may not reach orgasm unless they are orally stimulated. Another woman may need digital manipulation at the same time as her lover's penis thrusts in her vagina.

This variation has numerous subvariations: The woman may prefer her own fingers or she may prefer her lover's fingers. Some women prefer their lover's penis moving in a teasing shallow penetration so that it stimulates the vagina's sensitive pubococcygeal muscles. (However, it is difficult for younger men to achieve these shallow thrusts without quickly losing control of their ejaculation.) Others may prefer a swift or slow deep thrust so that the tip of the cervix is delicately touched. (Often this creates an exquisite sensation for both partners.)

Many women find the female superior position the best way to reach orgasm. There are several reasons for this. First, in that position a man can usually save energy and maintain an erection much longer. Second, astride a man, a woman can control the speed, angle, rhythm, and style of the thrusting, so she can choose whatever technique she feels most satisfying. But she must learn the optimum moment for changing over to that position. The best moment is when she is amply lubricated

and his penis is sufficiently erect. Also, she must be careful not to let the penis slip out of the vagina, for if she is not skillful enough to put it in again quickly the penis may lose its erection. And each time the penis has to reenter the vagina a considerable amount of lubrication may be lost.

In one variation of the female superior position, the woman turns around 180 degrees, facing the man's feet instead of his head. This position gives a woman a most advantageous opportunity to experiment with or to discover her G spot, first discovered by a man called Grafenberg in the middle of this century. It is a spot located inside the vagina between the pubic bone and the opening of the cervix (nearer to the pubic bone). Pressing this spot, as a rule, will give a pleasurable sensation. Today many researchers, including Wardell Pomeroy, director of the Institute for Advanced Study of Human Sexuality, believe that this spot may bring about a vaginal orgasm in a woman or even a type of ejaculating sensation when the woman is totally satisfied.

I have met many women who experience this ejaculatory sensation. Of course, the Tao discovered the female ejaculating phenomenon at least 2,000 years ago and called it *the tide of Yin.*

Almost all sexologists know that one of the worst enemies of a happy love relationship is anxiety. Exaggerated emphasis upon orgasm engenders anxiety, which often is the very obstacle to achieving it. The best way for a woman to reach orgasm is to learn to relax and enjoy all the pleasurable sensations of touching and thrusting, instead of laboriously struggling for an orgasm. As soon as a woman learns to enjoy the complete intimacy of body contact, her love-making will improve considerably.

Even if she does not achieve an orgasm, she will still enjoy making love. If her man has learned the Tao she will almost certainly be making love again within twenty-four hours. And in my experience, if a woman makes love often enough, she will not need orgasm every time. In fact, too many orgasms can be exhausting for some women. If both partners realize this, their relationship will immediately improve. On the other hand, struggling for orgasm will often spoil a love relationship.

THE EMPEROR'S NEW CLOTHES

For the last decade or more, our society has suffered from what I call "The Emperor's New Clothes" syndrome in its emphasis on spasmodic orgasm.

Many women admit confidentially that they have never experienced orgasm, but they enjoy making love immensely all the same. Many others do not experience orgasm but pretend to do so all the time. Still others reach orgasm regularly but do not really enjoy it and feel they have to pretend that they do. There are women who reach orgasm easily and truly enjoy it, and there are women who do not particularly care whether they reach orgasm or not as long as they have enough love-making, with endless variations.

The problem is that some men make women feel that they are abnormal unless they have an orgasm each time they make love. And many men will desert their women just because of that. The very word *orgasm* has caused endless suffering. The following are two true stories:

I met Frida five years ago, when she was a beautiful nineteen-year-old art student. She enjoyed making love as long and as often as possible. Three years ago she moved to the south of Sweden. She came to visit me last summer after an absence of two years. I asked her how her life was down south. I was surprised to learn that she had completely lost her appetite for making love. "Why?" I asked. Her answer was that nearly all the men she made love to in the south seemed unable to refrain from asking her the most horrible question: " 'Have you had an orgasm?' And I am so sick of hearing that repeatedly that I prefer not to make love with them at all!" These men gradually succeeded in killing her appetite for making love.

Lena is a voluptuous woman in her mid-thirties. Once I asked her to identify the worst lover she ever had. She had no difficulty singling out a man who persisted in asking her whether she had reached orgasm. He added that it was very important for him to know that, because he was determined to be a good lover! Lena can reach orgasm only after extremely prolonged, tender love-making, and that is beyond the capability of most men. She can, however, reach orgasm easily by masturbation, but she masturbates very rarely. She said she prefers by far to make love with a man without an orgasm than to have one by masturbation.

Frida and Lena are by no means isolated examples. A majority of the women I have discussed the subject with said they hated to be asked whether they were orgasmic. The exceptions were those who easily reach orgasm and who are very proud of the fact—but they are a very small minority.

Is a woman's orgasm necessary to her lover's highest pleasure? I think I can answer this question with a story from personal experience. About a year ago, I met a woman who might be called an orgasmic phenomenon. Maria could have up to fifty natural orgasms in an evening just by making love; she did not even require that her clitoris be touched with a finger. At first I was fascinated by her amazing orgasmic capability, for I had never met anyone quite like her before. Her orgasms came like bursts of volcanic fury, with loud, spasmodic screams.

After a few months of making love to her, however, my initial fascination disappeared. My enjoyment was not increased by her phenomenal ability. It was then that I realized that a woman's orgasm has very little to do with a man's pleasure in love-making. Then why do so many men insist that it is vital for their loving pleasure? It is because orgasm often appears to be the only visible or audible sign that a man has pleased a woman.

The criterion that truly matters is whether the woman is enjoying herself during love-making, with or without orgasm.

I am not saying that I did not enjoy making love with Maria; often, I did very much. I am only saying that after the novelty of her chain of orgasms wore off, it was not a vital factor in my loving enjoyment with her.

My most memorable love-making experiences are those in which I have found total communion with my partner. On these ecstatic occasions, neither of us have had to ask whether an orgasm had occurred.

NONDEMAND PLEASURING

It is no exaggeration to say that "chasing the orgasm" benefits neither women nor men. This orgasmic anxiety, along with the fear of unwanted pregnancy, has left many women with little enjoyment of love-making. Let us pay less attention to the term *orgasm*, which in the view of the Tao only confuses the issue and limits the most heavenly joy on earth.

Increasingly we read and hear such terms in sex therapy as nondemand coitus and nondemand pleasuring. Today nearly all sexologists are aware that fear is the worst enemy of loving pleasure, whether it is fear of performance or fear of failure. To counter such fears we should learn to enjoy loving in a relaxed, nondemanding way.

When one's love partner is laboriously trying to achieve an orgasm or to force an ejaculation, one should try to calm and to relax the partner by a soft, loving caress or, if necessary, by saying: "Don't worry about orgasm. The more you struggle, the more it will elude you. Just try to relax and enjoy yourself." Often this does help. In Mario Puzo's popular novel *Fools Die*, there is just such an example:

> One night in bed I couldn't quite get there. Not that I was impotent, but I couldn't finish. And she was trying like hell for me to make it. Finally she started to yell and scream....She was crying with frustration and failure....I laughed her out of it....I held her in my arms and we talked for a while and then after that we both came....*

The typical conception of many modern men and women is that without an ejaculation love-making is "unfinished."

ORGASM IS NOT ALWAYS NECESSARY

Orgasm becomes important and necessary only if we do not make love enough. The need for orgasm is somewhat like a very hungry person eating a big candy bar or a large dish of ice cream to kill the hunger. Today many people have learned that such eating habits are neither healthy nor truly satisfying. The most wholesome way to eat is to take a moderate portion whenever you feel slightly hungry and eat once again before you become very hungry.

Most people cannot achieve this in loving without learning the Tao. But once the Tao is mastered, it becomes extremely easy. For the Tao teaches a man how to control his ejaculation, and once a man learns this, he and his partner will be able to make love whenever one or both of them feels slightly hungry for loving.

After nearly half a century of observing and studying the subject, I have reached the conclusion that orgasms and ejaculations are necessary only for the sexually starved. For the not-so-hungry, each touch, caress, kiss, and loving thrust by a partner is a heavenly delight and a nourishing pleasure.

*Mario Puzo, *Fools Die* (London: Heinemann, 1978), p. 284.

Many women can enjoy their orgasm as a bonus whenever it comes their way. For most men the situation is quite different. They should learn to control their ejaculation, for whenever an ejaculation comes it temporarily terminates the love-making session. The man should ejaculate only when both partners feel that it is time for a pause. And he should not attempt ejaculation at every session. (For details, see the chapter "Ejaculation Control" in my first book, *The Tao of Love and Sex*.)

4. THE MONOGAMY MYTH

The Queen Mother of the West
Who has no husband but many healthy men
Using neither rouge nor powder,
She keeps herself healthy, young and beautiful.
What secret has she got?
Her secret is that of the Tao:
She eats very sparingly but loves very frequently.
She plays a lute,
And lets no trivia disturb
Her peace and harmony.

FROM *Yü Fan Pi Chü*

Are we all monogamous by nature? Far from it. Ava, whom I described in the first chapter, certainly is not. Neither are many other women and men I know. In an essay called "Polygyny and Polyandry," George Bernard Shaw promulgates the theory that our monogamous nature was a myth invented by inferior and insecure men who were alarmed by the fact that women did not like them. Instinctively women sought out the strongest, ablest men's seed to impregnate them so they would produce the best children. If a woman had to choose between a complete second-rate man and a fraction of a first-rate one, she would certainly prefer the latter. Second-rate and third-rate men created the law of monogamy so that they wouldn't be without women.

In his posthumously published *Letters from the Earth*, Mark Twain refers to the man who arbitrarily made the law of monogamy—without even consulting women, who have a dominant interest in the matter —as "this immeasurable hog."

If the well-known Sherfey theory, cited in the last chapter of this book, is to be believed, then prehistoric women were certainly far from monogamous. There are ample historical indications, too, that in ancient China neither women nor men were strictly monogamous. And only in that free atmosphere were the Taoists able to formulate the Tao of Loving to equalize the disparity in sexual capacity between men and women.

But this was to change drastically when the Confucians became politically dominant around the beginning of the first century. After that, women became virtually men's property; they lost the freedom to choose. But whenever a woman was in a position to choose, she was nearly always polygamous. Woo Chow, the only woman emperor in Chinese history, was an outstanding example. She was sixty-seven when she became emperor (she didn't call herself empress) and formed her own dynasty, which lasted only for the duration of her sixteen years in power. She had many male consorts and behaved exactly as an emperor.

The situation in the West was more or less the same. Cleopatra was an outstanding early example of a polygamous monarch. Even the Virgin Queen, Elizabeth I of England, was thought to have enjoyed many men in her life. Catherine the Great of Russia was of course even more famous for her fondness for numerous men.

In our era the situation has not changed much. Whenever a woman has power or wealth, she will do exactly as men do: She will be polygamous if she has the inclination, or polygamous in succession like Barbara Hutton, who married and divorced six times.

THE TAO'S THEORY

Monotony kills his desire.

SIMONE DE BEAUVOIR

Monotony kills her desire too, a fact that Madame de Beauvoir seems to have overlooked here, for in her books she has made it quite clear that she often had the desire for lovers other than Jean-Paul Sartre. I have heard many women (married or unmarried) say that whenever they see attrac-

tive men pass by they often wonder what it would be like to make love with them. None of us, regardless of sex and age, should feel ashamed of this natural tendency. Interest in the opposite sex is wholesome and necessary for a healthy and long life. In the last years of his life, Bernard Baruch (an adviser to FDR) said that he would be interested in attractive women as long as he lived.

All ancient books of the Tao stress the life-giving importance of natural stimulation from the opposite sex and the supreme importance of variation—of changes in sexual partners. If both love partners have equal rights and freedom, then "variation" doesn't sound so objectionable. Since most people are polygamous anyway—either in their minds or in reality—it would be futile to deny it.

What follows is a true story about the successful marriage of a Mr. and Mrs. Blank in the United States at the turn of the century. At first, because of her strict upbringing, Mrs. Blank tried to suppress her husband's outside love affairs. Their family atmosphere became frigid, tense, and explosive as a result. Finally Mrs. Blank realized that suppression was not the answer. She suggested that they try an experiment and grant each other equal freedom to have outside lovers. At first Mr. Blank would have none of it. He liked freedom for himself but he could not allow Mrs. Blank the right to other lovers. At last he relented in order to preserve the marriage, and the result was a complete success. Not only was the marriage saved, but they became much happier as a couple. Mrs. Blank eventually became an enthusiastic believer in this type of open marriage. It is a very interesting and inspiring story, told in Judge Ben Lindsey's book *The Companionate Marriage*.

Far too many people today suppress this natural need for variation. As a result, our hospital beds are filled with mentally and physically unhealthy people. It is true that some of us sublimate this natural desire, but the overwhelming majority go to the other extreme—toward excessive eating, drinking, and smoking or other forms of self-destruction.

It has been said that in medieval times sexual rivalry and jealousy were a major cause of violence. Loving and sex are a life-giving force of nature. It was the artificial restriction produced by taboos that caused much medieval violence. The *Tao Te Ching* says, "The more the taboos, the more miserable the people." The inevitable result of such prohibition and restriction is violence.

Ironically, this tragic waste, this unnecessary human suffering caused by love hunger, is completely man-made. Nearly everywhere on our planet objects of love and sex—men and women—are in ample supply, especially because *love is a very unusual thing in that the more we give and consume the more we will have.* If we could just liberate ourselves from such prejudices and taboos, and especially from the attitude that human beings are private property or chattel, then no one would have to suffer from this terrible love hunger.

And it can be done! Many people before us, famous and not so famous, have shown us how easily it can be done. Simone de Beauvoir has declared that she considers her experimental living arrangement with Jean-Paul Sartre the most significant accomplishment of her life. Not only did they never marry, but from the beginning they agreed to regard each other only as principal lovers. They both could have other intimate relationships whenever they felt the need and desire. And they accomplished that in an era when such arrangements were far more difficult than now. By almost any standard de Beauvoir and Sartre lived meaningfully, together or separately—at least, throughout most of their relationship.

Such open marriages, free from the double standard, have been a fact of life in America for a long time, even though more than ten years after *Open Marriage* became a bestseller, many states still have laws against the alternate lifestyles we are talking about.

And men must not think that it is weak to allow such arrangements. It is, on the contrary, courageous. You will be amply rewarded if you treat your lover or lovers with absolute equality. A woman will love you more and prefer you far more over those who regard her as private property or a prisoner. Ibsen's *Lady from the Sea* (published in 1888) tells the story of a young woman who is married to an older man. Several years after the marriage the woman's former lover comes back from the sea to reclaim her. She faces a hard decision about whether to leave or to stay, but two factors help make the choice easier: The wise older husband offers her love and complete freedom to make her own decision; the young sailor pressures her to follow him. She decides to stay. I read this play in Chinese translation when I was about thirteen and was very moved by it.

You may also have read a popular book called *The Collector*, by John Fowles. A collector of butterfly specimens meets a beautiful young girl and decides to treat her as he would a rare butterfly. He keeps her

locked in the cellar of an old house. In his own mad way he perhaps considers himself in love, but she soon dies in captivity.

These two stories tell us that human beings cannot be treated as property. Love can grow and prosper only in an atmosphere of harmony, equality, and freedom.

These examples are, of course, drawn from a playwright's and a novelist's imaginations. But real life too is filled with such examples. It is well known that Greta Garbo has chosen never to marry. She chose freedom instead; she wanted to enjoy free relationships with any man she pleased. In fact, she could be quite bold when she wanted to contact someone. She approached Gaylord Hauser, the noted dietician and author of *Look Younger, Live Longer*, with a simple telephone call. She was then thirty-three and popularly regarded as the most beautiful woman in the world. He was ten years older. The affair, which lasted only several months, was spoiled mainly by his desire to possess her by marriage. But they remained friends for many years afterward.

Garbo's relationship with her lover George Schlee lasted almost twenty years, until the latter's death. He was older and wiser than Hauser and knew how to keep their relationship alive. Garbo was forty when she met the sixty-year-old Schlee and was still regarded as the world's most beautiful woman. It is quite obvious why George Schlee succeeded where other men failed:

1. He was married and had no wish to divorce his wife.
2. He understood that Garbo did not wish to be anyone's wife.

SOME SWEDISH EXPERIMENTS

Experiments with free relationships between men and women occur frequently in Sweden. No statistics are yet available, but among my acquaintances the percentage of open relationships is very high. A young academic couple I know started off their relationship almost exactly like Simone de Beauvoir and Jean-Paul Sartre. They have been happily married for five years. The wife has many more affairs than the husband. At her husband's request, she occasionally brings a new lover home to meet him, and often the men establish a lasting friendship. Some of her husband's closest friends are her former lovers.

An attractive thirty-six-year-old public servant I know remained a virgin until she was thirty-one, when she met a man who interested her. It was like a sudden awakening from a bad dream. She realized that she had wasted many of her best years. She vowed to make up for those dull years by fully occupying herself with public sex education and with interesting men so that her spare evenings would never be wasted again. She is now one of the busiest women I know.

But the following example is most unusual because there are many children involved. One couple met another couple about ten years older during a vacation, and the four became very close friends. Then after awhile, almost simultaneously, each of the four found the other's spouse very attractive. With their husbands' approval, the two women worked out a system of switching husbands every two weeks or so without disturbing their four children (two in each family). Their in-laws disliked the shockingly novel idea, but their children seem to get along very well with their additional fathers.

LIBERATION FROM HYPOCRISY

I love roast beef,
But I don't want it every day.

MAGGIE TEYTE

Maggie Teyte, the famous British singer at the turn of the century, was actually most famous in France. She was the favorite of Claude Debussy, who composed the opera *Pelleas et Melisande* especially for her. Soon after her divorce Teyte was asked by interviewers whether she planned to remarry. The above quotation was her answer.

The Tao arrives at a similar conclusion: Marriage is a fine institution if it is kept flexible and open; otherwise staleness and boredom will eventually erode the union. One must not watch one's mate like a warden. Individuals, of course, are all slightly different from each other. Some people flourish gloriously in monogamy, while others thrive only in freer relationships. A truly free society should be able to accommodate all life patterns.

As long as each of us respects the rights and inclinations of others and does not apply any form of pressure or coercion to others, we should all have the right to live our private lives in whatever form we choose. I am happy to say that in most parts of the Western world this is already a fact.

François Mauriac, winner of the Nobel Prize for Literature in 1952, once described himself as a combination of all the women in his life. That description might have come from the heart of a Taoist. All of us, men and women, are a mosaic formed by the total of our love experiences.

The renowned French actress Jeanne Moreau was once asked about her dreams. One of her fantasies was to have a huge, beautiful house with numerous apartments in it. Each of the apartments would house one of her lovers, past or present, so that she could visit them regularly whenever she wished.

Today, of course, many people still live under puritanical strictures and they expect their mates, married or unmarried, to remain pure when they are absent, no matter how long. They do not seem to realize that loneliness is unhealthy and that it benefits no one. And their mate's health and happiness are far more important than keeping a promise of fidelity.

JUNG'S ADVICE TO HUSBANDS AND WIVES

The prerequisite for a good marriage
Is the license to be unfaithful.

CARL GUSTAV JUNG

Few people in history have enjoyed so much respect in and out of their own countries during their lifetime and after as Carl Gustav Jung (1875–1961). He was known as The Sage of Zurich in that very straitlaced financial capital of Switzerland. By any standard, his marriage of fifty-two years to Emma Rauschenbach was a success. And he cried when she died: "She was a queen! She was a queen!" But theirs was by no means a monogamous union.

The second most important woman in Jung's life was the elegant Toni Wolff, who came to him as a patient when she was twenty-two and later became his pupil, inspiration, and intimate friend. Thirteen years

younger than Jung, she became a practicing analyst herself and lived in a huge, luxurious flat with marble pillars. Their relationship lasted until she died, forty-three years later.

Jung's wife, Emma, also became a practicing analyst. Whether both women had other affairs is not known. Perhaps they did, but in a city of double standards like Zurich, they would have had to keep their affairs secret.

Jung and Emma's long marriage produced five children—four girls and a boy. Jung wrote Freud that he tried "every conceivable trick to stem the tide of these little blessings." But perhaps his wife wanted many children.

The next longest relationship Jung had was with an Englishwoman named Ruth Bailey. They met in Africa and she moved into his house as his companion until he died at eighty-five. The relationship lasted more than thirty-five years.

THE IMPORTANCE OF CHANGE

After a man has mastered the Tao
The only thing he has to worry about
Is not making love frequently enough!

FROM *Yü Fang Chi Tao*

When Louis XV of France was in his forties, his health began to fail. "It is said that the king's doctor warned him that he was making love too often. 'But you told me I could, as much as I wanted to, so long as I use no aphrodisiacs.' 'Ah, sir! Change is the greatest aphrodisiac of all!'"

The word "change" as used by the king's doctor refers to numerous changes in love partners, and the doctor was quite right in saying that change is the greatest aphrodisiac of all. The ancient Tao masters knew this thousands of years ago.

Is change physically harmful? Not if you have learned the Tao. I don't recommend artificial or medical aphrodisiacs, but some change from time to time (I don't mean a divorce or a break with one's love partner) can be rejuvenating for almost anyone. Monotony and boredom are the worst enemies of many marriages and relationships. So long as all parties concerned agree, I can see no harm in new partners. Frequent lovemaking for both men and women plays a key role in the Tao's secret of youth. And to maintain optimum frequency of love-making, change is often necessary!

5. OBSTACLES TO LEARNING TO LOVE

EMPEROR HUANG TI: *What will happen to those misinformed young men who ejaculate three or even five times daily to show off their strength?*

SU NÜ: *If they squander their strength so drastically beyond their means, they will soon exhaust their power. Impotence will be an inevitable result. If they go on like this unchecked they may not live long!*

FROM *Su Nü Miao Lun*
CHAPTER 7

In these sexually liberated times, with so much talk about love and sex, why do so many people have sexual difficulties? Can it be that some modern sexologists have added to those problems?

MISINFORMATION

The more the taboos,
The more miserable the people.

FROM *Tao Te Ching*
CHAPTER 57

In almost no other human endeavor is there more misinformation than in the area of love and sex between man and woman. Centuries of taboos have certainly contributed greatly to this miserable situation. Not surprisingly, in China the soundest advice on the subject was formulated before the Confucianists came to power. In the West the situation is just the reverse. The censors and the hypocrites have only recently begun to loosen their grip, and books of true value on sexual matters began to appear only during this century.

GALEN

We should of course give some credit to the second-century Greek physician Galen, who paid a great deal of attention to the subject. He correctly observed that the absence of sexual relations could cause hysterical symptoms; but he incorrectly went on to say that retention of sperm contributes to psychic imbalance and anxiety. He called attention to the fatigue and exhaustion that may follow sexual activity,* but he did not realize that his own theory may have contributed greatly to this fatigue and exhaustion. And his theory may indeed have caused countless men through the centuries to become preoccupied with their own ejaculations.

Galen's theory about retention of sperm, and those of others who have followed in his footsteps, has cast a long and unfortunate shadow on man–woman relationships. According to the Tao, sperm should not be retained indefinitely, but neither should it be squandered. Emissions of sperm should be controlled according to age, physical condition, and so on. (For details on this subject see *The Tao of Love and Sex*, Chapter 3.)

What I must add here is that if a man follows Galen's advice—*ejaculating whenever he makes love*—and does not heed the advice of the Tao—*keeping his ejaculation in reasonable and rhythmatic control according to his own personal need*—several dissatisfying consequences will result:

1. Coition will be over too quickly. This may give some relief but no true satisfaction, for the man simply had not enough time to enjoy and sa-

*Norman Sussman, M.D., "Sex and Sexuality in History," in Sadock et al., eds., *The Sexual Experience* (Baltimore: William & Wilkins, 1976), p. 19.

vor the experience. Love-making will be over after one short, tense, and nervous session. That is why this type of love-making often is called combat; and its aftermath is perhaps the emotional exhaustion Galen described.

2. Unless a woman is able to reach orgasm quickly, this type of love-making will leave her hanging in the air, highly dissatisfied. If the man is sensitive he will usually see his partner's dilemma, which adds to his own frustration. So he tries to help with his fingers. Some women may like that, but some may not. A more virile man may attempt coition once again after a respite. But if he has no knowledge of the Tao he will once more be preoccupied with his ejaculation, which, though usually slower than the first, may happen again quickly. Many men do not have a natural urge to have a second ejaculation, so they usually have to force it—and the result is even worse. The man is fatigued and sadder than before.

On the other hand, *if a man follows the Tao's way rather than the teaching of Galen*, these pleasing results will occur:

1. He will not preoccupy himself with ejaculation.

2. He will concentrate on the most ecstatic sensation in the world—that deriving from his body's intimate contact with his lover.

3. When he is thrusting and touching, the heavenly sensations will reach several plateaus, peaks, and ebbs. In the view of the Tao, each such peak is much more enjoyable than any ejaculation.

4. The Tao's way of love-making usually ends in a fusion of the two lovers, who embrace and caress each other for a while the penis until slowly drops out of the vagina. As a rule, women prefer this way of loving far more than what Galen has prescribed. Simone de Beauvoir has said in *The Second Sex* that a woman's sexuality hardly ever ends and that it flows like waves through peaks and valleys into infinity. When a man has mastered the Tao, his sexuality is more or less like that of his woman. Under such favorable conditions, true fusion is possible. And the partners can have as many love-making sessions as they wish. For

when a man has truly mastered the Tao, love-making will rarely lead to fatigue.

After coitus all animals are sad
Except women and cocks.

Galen is credited with the above witty observation. In my opinion this observation is not accurate. None of the animals I have observed—lions, horses, dogs, goats, ducks, sparrows, and so on—ever showed signs of sorrow after coition. Perhaps we human beings are the only animals that are often sad after love-making.

Desmond Morris, author of *The Naked Ape*, describes "man" humorously in a similar vein:

> This unusual and highly successful species spends a great deal of time examining his high motives and an equal amount of time studiously ignoring his fundamental ones. He is proud that he has the biggest brain of all the primates, but attempts to conceal the fact that he also has the biggest penis.*

Until now most human beings have remained quite ignorant of their own loving potential. We human beings are able to make love more frequently and sensuously than perhaps any other animal. Yet we are often disappointed after love-making. Why? Because most of us are like owners of a precious Stradivarius violin that we have never learned to play. Each of us possesses a body that is unique among all animals—we have smooth, sensitive, and almost hairless skin which is able to give and receive pleasure that is all but incomparable.

Often I tell friends that sometimes I feel a little envious when I see how freely and gracefully birds fly and how convenient it is that both birds and animals have their handsome coats of fur and feathers that are good for all climates and seasons. But when I see how clumsily and monotonously they make love, I feel very lucky to have my smooth and sensitive skin.

It is indeed tragic that many of us never even know what loving pleasure we can have. At the beginning of his brief memoir *The Facts of*

---

*Desmond Morris, *The Naked Ape* (London: Corgi Books, 1968), p. 9.

Life, the Scottish psychiatrist R. D. Laing says: "My father was the only one in his family to marry and, with one possible exception, the only one ever to commit sexual intercourse."*

You may say that this is just an odd incident which could happen only in Scotland at the first half of our century. It may surprise you that even in Sweden today many obviously healthy young men simply do not make love. Only a few days ago I had an intimate conversation with a handsome young scientist in his early thirties and in normal physical condition who has never even kissed a woman. He has a natural longing for women, but the mere thought of approaching them intimately paralyzes him. He masturbates about once a week. If he does not do that, he will have a wet dream about once a month. Several times during his travels he has received homosexual overtures, which have disgusted him. He is celibate.

These love problems are man-made! No one needs to fear making love. And no one needs to be sad after coition. On the contrary, all of us ought to be happy and inspired both before and after making love.

VAN DE VELDE

If a man wishes to live a long and healthy life
He must learn how to love and how to treasure
    his sperm.
Also learn how to breathe and to relax.
And how to eat correctly.

PÊNG TSU

To us, Galen's influence is profound but not direct, for today only very few researchers of medical history read his original texts. Van de Velde's influence is quite a different matter. His book *Ideal Marriage*, first published in 1928, has been translated into many languages and has sold millions of copies. The merit of his book is that it ushered people out of the Victorian age and made them somewhat less hypocritical in matters of love and sex. This virtue, however, has been almost completely overshadowed by Van de Velde's dogmatic insistence that a man ejaculate every time he makes

*R. D. Laing, *The Facts of Life* (London: Penguin, 1977), p. 9

love. He utters "an urgent warning"* against making love without ejaculation. His belief, like Galen's, is the direct opposite of the Tao. His warning has been repudiated by modern research, particularly the work of Masters and Johnson.† But the insistence on ejaculation continues to have a tragic aftermath. Many men and women still consider it abnormal or at least incomplete to make love without ejaculation.

DAVID REUBEN AND ALEX COMFORT

If you believe in every book,
It is better there is no book at all!

ANCIENT CHINESE PROVERB

Even though Master and Johnson's books on love and sex were bestsellers during the latter half of the 1960s and in the 1970s, they were read mainly by the professionals, because they are written in technical language that is not easy for the layman to understand. In those years the majority of those who wished to know more about love and sex read popular books by David Reuben and Alex Comfort.

Dr. Reuben's books on love and sex are amusing and contain some good information. But readers of Reuben must be wary. In his most popular book, *Everything You Always Wanted to Know About Sex*, he makes many questionable statements. In my first book I repudiated a few of his remarks; others have been criticized in Chapter 6 of this volume.

Alex Comfort's two books about sex are still quite popular in the United States today, especially *The Joy of Sex*. When I first saw them, my immediate reaction was quite favorable. I was impressed by such sound advice as "Don't give her a vibrator . . . it's inclined to damp down sensitivity with prolonged use,"** and "Also, if you use [anal intercourse,] don't mix it with straight vaginal intercourse—this leads to troublesome infections in some people with yeast and other organisms which belong in

---

*H. Van de Velde, *Ideal Marriage* (London: Heinemann, 1965), p. 79.
†William Masters and Virginia Johnson, *Human Sexual Inadequacy* (Boston: Little, Brown, 1970), chapter 12.
**Alex Comfort, *More Joy of Sex* (New York: Simon & Schuster, 1975), p. 66.

the gut, not in the vagina or the male urethra."* I bought both books for thorough reading in Stockholm.

In the preface to *The Joy of Sex*, Comfort says: "It must be the first sex counseling book to be properly researched."† Naturally I checked his accuracy by seeing what he had to say about the "Chinese style" of lovemaking,** for that is one subject I do know. To say that I was amazed by what I found is to put it very politely and mildly. He just brushes it aside, almost exactly as Van de Velde did some fifty years earlier. This discovery of course dampened my confidence in his research, and I decided to check further by a very careful reading. I found the following excerpt from a chapter called "Come Again":

> With men it is complicated still. Some can get six or more full orgasms in a few hours provided they aren't time-stressed and don't attempt it daily. Others can do it daily. Others cannot get a second erection for a set time. It pays to establish this time early on—it may be shorter than you think. Whether it is alterable nobody knows—nor yet whether individual differences depend on physical or mental factors, though certainly a great many men have been hocussed by talk about sex being exhausting into a performance below what they could manage. . . . Since exercise and practice improve almost all performances, it would be odd if they didn't improve this one. . . .‡

With some rare exceptions all men who have much experience in life and love know that it is not making love but ejaculation that is exhausting. A woman friend of mine once had a lover who could ejaculate six times or more in an evening. But what was the point? Those ejaculations made neither of them happy. According to her: "Afterward, he was like a squeezed lemon, almost dead!"

The last sentence of Comfort's above advice can be most harmful if a man takes it seriously, without knowing which is the correct and which is the harmful form of "exercise and practice." Increasing the capacity to ejaculate will lead only to eventual impotence, temporary or permanent. The Tao has thousands of years of wisdom on this subject. Masters and

*Alex Comfort, *The Joy of Sex* (New York: Simon & Schuster, 1974), p. 118.
†*Ibid.*, p. 1.
***Ibid.*, pp. 130–131.
‡*Ibid*, pp. 26–27.

Johnson's *Human Sexual Inadequacy* (Chapter 12) also discusses "forced ejaculation."

If you wish further information, you might read an article by Donald S. Marshall, "Sexual Behavior on Mangaia," a study of inhabitants of the South Sea island of Mangaia, where men not only "exercise and practice" to increase their sexual capability, but even compete to see who can have the most women in one day. And here is the warning:

> But there is little doubt that many Mangaian males pay a biological penalty for this social cultural fact: That is, the Mangaian male is probably far more subject to impotence and sterility in later years than is the American male. He is subject to "tira," a condition in which the penis changes in its ability to rise and react. . . . *

In the same chapter, Comfort does give a good piece of information: "Most overfast responders are having sex far too rarely." But again he spoils it a little later by saying: "Vigorous masturbation will always produce a second ejaculation in time, even if it doesn't produce a serviceable erection."†

Another of Alex Comfort's favorite subjects is masturbation. In the Victorian age boys and girls were severely punished for playing with themselves. We even hear stories about little boys' hands being tied or even connected to alarm devices during sleep. Now of course the pendulum has swung the other way. Comfort, for example, writes: "If your daughter doesn't masturbate, there would be a case for teaching her. . . ."** That, I think, is going to the extreme. What young people need today is a complete education in making love safely and enjoyably, not in masturbation.

I am not at all against masturbation and I do not regard it as a sin or evil; in fact, I think it is horrible to feel guilty because one has masturbated. But I am of the same view as Wardell Pomeroy, a former associate of Kinsey, that masturbation can never take the place of love-making.

---

*Donald S. Marshall and Robert C. Suggs, "Sexual Behavior on Mangaia," *Human Sexual Behavior*, P. Feldman and M. MacCulloch, eds. (New York: John Wiley & Sons, 1980), p. 160.
†Comfort, *The Joy of Sex*, p. 29.
**Comfort, *More Joy of Sex*, p. 66.

Desmond Morris, in the introduction to his second book, *The Human Zoo*, said: "Under normal conditions, in their natural habitats, wild animals do not mutilate themselves, masturbate, attack their offspring, develop stomach ulcers...or form homosexual pair-bonds. Among human city dwellers, needless to say, all of these things occur." * Although masturbation, homosexuality, and stomach ulcers are part of today's reality, we can hardly imagine consciously teaching our children how to be homosexuals or how to develop stomach ulcers—so why should we teach our daughters to masturbate?

After forty-three years of studying the problems between men and women, I can say with little doubt that when a man becomes too used to masturbation, he will often feel that he cannot be bothered looking for a woman. He can also become a less adequate lover both for his partner and himself, for he is conditioned to the stimulation of his own hand. Similarly, when a woman becomes too used to masturbation, her clitoris may lose its delicate sensitivity and she may have difficulty achieving orgasm without finger stimulation.

I should add that we do not need to interfere with our children's masturbation once they have already acquired the habit. For if they are taught the correct way of loving, sooner or later they will stop masturbating. Through the years numerous men and woman have told me that as soon as they learned the pleasure and harmony of true loving they stopped masturbation completely, or practiced it only out of necessity.

Masturbation is a poor substitute, and we should treat it as a last resort when no love partner is available. To masturbate is a lonely endeavor, devoid of human warmth, contact, and communication. In the language of the Tao, it lacks the harmony of Yin and Yang. After years of masturbation, many men and women become recluses without contact with the other sex.

* Desmond Morris, *The Human Zoo* (London: Corgi Books, 1971), p. 9.

6. BIRTH CONTROL AND THE TAO

UNWANTED PREGNANCY ENGENDERS HATRED

"God damn you, Morris, you bastard!"

MARILYN FRENCH

The above quotation is from a maternity ward scene in Marilyn French's popular novel *The Women's Room.** It is a familiar scene. Unwanted pregnancies can cause bitter hatred between men and women. And the children accidentally produced are often not loved.

In the same book there is another expressive passage: "Good Christ, the way everybody has them! Accidents, my three little accidents. . . ."† Just two days ago I talked with a Stockholm girl who told me that as far as she knew her parents' five children were all accidents!

---

*Marilyn French, *The Women's Room* (London: Andre Deutsch, 1978), p. 51.
†*Ibid.*, p. 117.

METHODS DISCREDITED AND REINSTATED

I am inclined to believe that the widespread use of the pill poses a serious metabolic threat to our society. Something that so profoundly affects the hormonal balance of women cannot be completely safe.

RENE DUBOS

The above is the opinion of the well-known French-born American microbiologist.* For years Sweden has rivaled the United States in the number of contraceptive pill users per capita. In spite of this, all the women physicians I know have been prudent enough not to take the pill themselves. A woman scientist who directs a research laboratory in one of Sweden's largest hospitals told me: "In our lab, we are using estrogen to induce cancerous tumors in mice—do you think I would be mad enough to take the pill myself that is mainly made of estrogen?"

As early as 1969 England's prestigious medical journal *Lancet* had this to say about the pill in an editorial:

> The metabolic changes associated with this treatment may modify biochemical processes in all body tissues. More than 50 metabolic changes have been recorded. . . . These changes are unnecessary for contraception and their ultimate effect on the health of the user is unknown. . . . The wisdom of administering such compounds to healthy women for many years must be seriously questioned.†

In the United States the *New England Journal of Medicine* said almost the same thing in 1976:

> The pill abolishes the normal cycle, distorts metabolism, and causes serious disorder in some cases. . . . The whole question of the use of drugs to alter normal metabolism must be raised.**

---

*René Dubos, *Horizon*, Summer 1970, p. 61.
†As quoted in the preface of Barbara Seaman and Gideon Seaman, *Women and the Crises of Sex Hormones* (New York: Rawson, 1977).
**Ibid.

Thanks to these warnings, many women have stopped taking the pill. Nowadays, physicians too are much more cautious in prescribing it. The IUD too has been called into question. During the last few years Swedish doctors have all but stopped inserting IUDs into young women's uteruses because of numerous cases of infections. IUDs have been known to cause copious and prolonged bleeding during menstruation, and the nylon string left outside the cervix for checking and retrieving the IUD can irritate the penis of the man making love with the woman.

So now the once lowly condom has become less unthinkable and unpopular, and some doctors go as far as calling it the King of Contraception. Condoms, if used properly, do have several virtues. They are relatively cheap, easy to obtain, and free of side effects. They also prevent infections.

NO ACCIDENT IN OVER FORTY-FOUR YEARS

I gave much thought to the subject of contraception even before I started making love. In those days in China, condoms and diaphragms had already become available. But as a believer in nature's wisdom, I chose the natural method of withdrawal. Unfortunately, I had also read H. Van de Velde's *Ideal Marriage*, which instrumentally delayed my practicing ejaculation control according to the Tao for twelve years. It also cast a shadow of doubt in my mind about practicing withdrawal, a technique Van de Velde warned against.*

Luckily, I eventually asked Fang Tien, a Taoist colleague of mine during World War II, this important question. Fang Tien was almost twenty years older than I, and we both served the commander-in-chief of the southern half of China in the scenic city of Kweilin. Fang was a senior officer; I was a junior. But because we both loved to ride horses during siren-free cloudy days (to avoid being caught by air raids), we became rather intimate friends. He introduced me to his charming wife, who was then about thirty-five, and their two teenage sons. During one of our riding sessions we took a break near one of the beautiful caves for which Kweilin is famous. As we sat down I brought up the subject:

*H. Van de Velde, *Ideal Marriage* (London: Heinemann, 1965), pp. 166–168.

"Can I ask you a personal question?"

"Of course."

"How did you manage to have just these two sons and no more?"

"Very simple. I no longer give my wife my semen."

"You mean you use a contraceptive device?"

"Who really needs any of those stupid things!"

"You mean you practice coitus interruptus? But isn't that method supposed to be bad for the nerves?"

"No, not at all, and you shouldn't call it by that name. Call it withdrawal. If you want to be a good lover, you should first learn never to interrupt. What I mean is that you should ejaculate only when your love partner has been totally satisfied. Ejaculation before she is completely satisfied is an interruption to her, and that can be bad for her nerves. But if you have learned how to satisfy her thoroughly, she will not suffer at all from your withdrawal."

"What about accidents?"

"Well, I have practiced this with my wife for about fifteen years and you can see for yourself that we did not have any accidents. The two boys came as we planned. My wife and I have lived in Europe for five years, and I often told my European friends that all those contraceptive devices were unnecessary except perhaps for the condom, which can help prevent diseases."

I practiced withdrawal the very first time I made love, at the beginning of 1938. In more than forty-four years I have not used any other contraceptive method and I have not had a single accident. For years many skeptics claimed that I was safe because I was not man enough to impregnate any woman; they refused to give credit to the effectiveness of the withdrawal method. Not until I did have children—a boy in 1971 and a girl in 1972—did such sarcastic remarks cease, for they proved that I am at least as fertile as the average man.

I do not know exactly why the withdrawal method has been so unpopular with American doctors. Possibly because in the United States mechanical devices have been highly respected in almost every aspect of life during the last hundred years. For example, David Reuben, author of *Everything You Always Wanted to Know About Sex*, says that the withdrawal method "is better than nothing—but not much better."* According to Dr. Reuben, exactly one spermatozoon is needed to get a woman pregnant. That is not quite correct. It is common knowledge today that even though only one spermatozoon actually fertilizes the ovum, the cooperation of a vast number is necessary for impregnation. A spermatozoon is much smaller and frailer than the ovum, and before one can penetrate an ovum, a vast number of spermatozoa must release an enzyme called hyaluronidase, which weakens the ovum's outer protective layer.

According to Dr. Reuben, the risk of pregnancy with the withdrawal method is very great because "there are always a few drops of secretion in the penis; each drop contains about 50,000 sperm. If they leak into the vagina, one drop is more than enough to make an egg into a baby."† This theory too does not hold up in light of today's knowledge. It is commonly known today that a man with a sperm count of fewer than 20 million will generally be infertile. If 20 million sperm cannot do the job, how can 50,000 succeed?

The authors of a more recent book, *The Ms Medical Guide to a Woman's Health*, call withdrawal "a difficult and distressing method." They still hold to David Reuben's theory. They have, however, made progress by mentioning the importance of the man's urinating after each ejaculation to clear the urethra of sperm before making love again when practicing the withdrawal method. But even here they have presented the subject in a misleading manner: "Another problem with the method is the fact that intercourse cannot occur again until the man urinates, which may be up to several hours."**

Having practiced the withdrawal method thousands of times for over forty years and discussed it with many men who also practice it successfully, I can emphatically say that this is hardly a problem. First, very few men will have the energy or urge to resume intercourse quickly after ejaculation; even a very strong and virile man will usually pause for at least thirty minutes before resuming coition. And during that period,

*David Reuben, *Everything You Always Wanted to Know About Sex* (New York: Avon Books, 1971), p. 247.
† *Ibid.*
**Excerpted in *Ms* magazine, September 1979.

unless the man drinks too little liquid or is too lazy to go to the toilet, he will have no difficulty whatsoever in urinating at least once. I always urinate soon after ejaculation and again just before resuming intercourse, and each time I thoroughly wash with water, without soap. Perhaps this is an important factor in my not having had a single accident in forty-four years. Is it difficult to urinate twice in thirty minutes? Not at all, after a little practice.

I should make it clear that I am not trying to persuade anyone to practice the withdrawal method. Each couple must make up their own minds and assume joint responsibility for contraception. But men should realize that women have shouldered the burden of contraception virtually alone for too long. The task endangers many women's health and in some cases even their lives. This subject has caused considerable animosity and disharmony between the sexes.

IS WITHDRAWAL A DIFFICULT METHOD?

I made love for the first time when I was eighteen and practiced withdrawal from the beginning. It was a clean withdrawal, no mess and no accident, but in those early days I could hardly call that very satisfying love-making. My lover was one year older and also a virgin. I courted her for over a year before she consented to make love. Previously we had spent two nights together, but she wanted to keep her virginity so she allowed me only to hug and caress her. You can imagine the bottled-up passion ready to explode when I penetrated her hymen. I did manage to enter the threshold but I had to make a swift, instant withdrawal.

Was it difficult? For me it was not difficult. Because I understood that it was almost a sacred duty for a man not to cause an unwanted pregnancy. I have encountered only one man, a not-so-bright young truck driver, who did not respect this duty. He boasted that he had a baby in every town he frequented.

The fact is that the withdrawal method played an important role in the early historical decline in birth rates among the people of Northern and Western Europe. Moreoever, failure rates with the withdrawal method have been comparatively low in several studies. In a lecture delivered at the Fifteenth Nobel Symposium for the Control of Human Fertility, C. Tietze of the Population Council in New York said:

> If [withdrawal] is "correctly practiced," withdrawal of the penis from the vagina is accomplished prior to ejaculation. . . . The method would have to be classified as highly effective. However, many males are physiologically unable to practice coitus interruptus correctly, either because they do not perceive the imminence of ejaculation or because they cannot withdraw in time.*

In fact, very few men are unfit to practice the withdrawal method. Exceptions include those who are physically and mentally impaired; those who are unable to perceive the imminence of ejaculation; and those whose will prevents them from carrying out the determination to withdraw. Such men should not practice withdrawal.

A woman who does not like artificial contraceptives can carry out a simple test to determine if her lover is capable of practicing withdrawal effectively. She can suggest that her lover use a condom in the beginning to see if he is able to start ejaculation after withdrawal instead of before. After a few such successful tests, the couple can choose a relatively safe period just before or just after the woman's menstruation to practice withdrawal without a condom.

HOW TO PRACTICE WITHDRAWAL CORRECTLY

If the withdrawal method is "correctly practiced," it is indeed highly effective. To practice it correctly, a man must withdraw from the vagina before ejaculation. This requires:

1. Learning to perceive clearly the signs that precede ejaculation.

2. Learning to withdraw swiftly and to be a little too early rather than too late.

*Control of Human Fertility (The Topic of Nobel Symposium 15), p. 311; edited by Professors Egon Diczfalusy and Ulf Borell of the University of Stockholm, 1971.

3. Learning ejaculation control as described in my first book, *The Tao of Love and Sex.*

In this manner a man can effectively eliminate distress for both partners. In fact, if ejaculation control and withdrawal are combined, not only is distress eliminated but the man becomes a much more effective, successful, and happy lover. Now both he and his partner are truly liberated in love-making.

I have found the following sequence highly effective in love-making:

1. Before making love, a man should urinate and wash his penis thoroughly with warm water without soap (most soaps are too alkaline and can cause irritation). Our skin surface is protected by unsaturated fatty acids, which inhibit the growth of several bacterial and fungal cutaneous pathogens.* This normally acid surface should not be neutralized by alkaline soap, since irritations or even infections may result. If the man feels his penis needs a special washing, he might use a little liquid shampoo, which is usually neutral instead of alkaline. Of course, if he wishes to spend a little money he can buy a bottle of liquid acid soap of pH 3.5 at a pharmacy for washing his private parts.

Urination and thorough washing reduce the chances of transmitting pathogens to the vagina. At the same time, they can prolong the duration of love-making. A large quantity of urine in the bladder will hasten a man's urge to ejaculate. If a man urinates more frequently, he will feel much more at ease in controlling his ejaculation. Even if he does not ejaculate, he should go to the toilet about once an hour during sex to reduce the urge to ejaculate. This practice can also eliminate those leaking drops of sperm that David Reuben and many others are so worried about.

*Mary J. Marples, "Life on the Human Skin," *Scientific American*, January 1969, p. 115.

2. A man should determine where and on what to ejaculate when he withdraws so that he will not make a mess of the sheets. Usually if a man ejaculates neatly and cleanly, he can save on the laundry bill. In my early years I used a little towel as a receptacle for my sperm. As years passed my control and withdrawal became more expert. Now I usually deposit the sperm on my partner's navel. This has the added advantage of allowing the woman to see and feel that the withdrawal has been done cleanly. As a result, her confidence in her love partner's ability will usually increase.

At this stage both partners should go to the bathroom to wash, without soap. Both must urinate first before washing. For the man, this will not only reduce the incidence of urinary infection and trichomoniasis infestation, it will also make him safer for his woman. For the woman too, this urination will reduce the incidence of infection.

3. If caressing resumes after a certain pause (say, twenty or thirty minutes, or even longer) and the man wishes to reenter his partner, he should go to the bathroom again to urinate and wash his penis. This will doubly ensure against pregnancy.

4. If a man ejaculates for a second time during an evening, he should repeat the urination and washing as after the first ejaculation.

If the man has read my first book, *The Tao of Love and Sex*, and has learned ejaculation control, he will ejaculate less and less as time passes. I now ejaculate every one or two months, so I withdraw *and* ejaculate only a few times a year. I sincerely believe that there is no better contraceptive method for a man who practices the Tao.

CONCLUSION

The man who practices withdrawal must assume full responsibility and remain in perfect control. During the deepest moments of passion, his love partner may urge him not to withdraw. Afterward, however, she will regret it. So if the man cannot remain in control at such moments, it is better for him not to practice withdrawal.

For true practitioners of the Tao, the problems of contraception no longer exist.

7. THE IMPORTANCE OF TEACHING LOVING

I am no good at love,
Because I did not love my mother.

RILKE

What Rilke sadly realized is rather common knowledge today. Still, very few people take such words seriously and believe them wholeheartedly. When a mother or would-be mother is convinced of the absolute importance of the relationship between her and her future child, she will do something to ensure the success of that relationship.

WHAT CAN BE DONE?

There are at least seven points a potential mother should keep in mind:

1. Do not let yourself conceive unless you truly want a child.

2. Refrain from forming a strong preconceived preference for having either a son or a daughter.

3. If you do not succeed in remaining impartial, do your utmost to keep your preference strictly to yourself. There is almost nothing more damaging to the relationship as this information. It could gravely wound your child's self-confidence.

4. For the same reason, you must refrain from dressing your boy like a girl or your girl like a boy.

5. If you have more than one child, treat them all with scrupulous fairness and equality; keep favoritism strictly out of your family.

6. Do not beat your children in any way, but firmly and unwaveringly carry out your warnings or promises.

7. Practice as much touching and holding as both parties can enjoy. Do your utmost to keep jealousy from forming. Jealousy between either mother and daughter or father and son can easily spoil the harmonious atmosphere.

OUR MOTHERS STARTED TEACHING US
EVEN BEFORE WE WERE BORN

When she is pregnant, she must do the following:
She must practice good deeds
She must not look at ugly colors
She must not listen to ugly sounds or voices
She must not use bad language
She must not be frightened or worried
She must not overwork to tire herself
She must eat very carefully and thoughtfully
She must not ride horses or climb mountains
She must not walk too fast
She must read good books and listen to beautiful music
The above are just some important points of what we call:
To teach the young when they are still in a mother's womb.

FROM *Tung Hsüan Tzu*

Thus most women in ancient China began their careers as natural teachers. Historically, nearly all men and women of accomplishment had good teachers as their mothers. But even among this select group, few have been equipped with the correct technical knowledge of loving (otherwise our world would be in a much healthier condition). For those who haven't read my first book, I'll provide a brief review of the Tao's view on these matters:

1. The importance of technique in almost every aspect of life cannot be exaggerated. Balzac humorously describes the average man's inept effort at making love to a woman as "an orangutan that tries to play a violin." Although technique alone will never make a great violinist, sound technique is a necessary ingredient for excellence. Similarly, an adequate lover or effective teacher in loving must first be equipped with adequate technique; otherwise success is impossible.

2. The superb pleasure of physical love is a natural antidote for all the unpleasant aspects of life. The better the quality and the more the quantity of loving we have, the happier our lives will be.

WHAT SHOULD THE YOUNG BE TAUGHT IN LOVING?

As I have said previously, I would certainly not teach the young how to masturbate—simply because there is no need. Children generally start to masturbate far earlier than adults ever imagine. My boy, for example, started to play with his little penis when he was only a year old, and it is amazing that he managed to have perfect erections.

What boys and girls need to be taught effectively is natural birth control. Boys in particular must be impressed with the extreme importance of learning how to control their ejaculations so they will have a natural form of birth control when they begin to engage in love-making.

After reading my first book, a Stockholm manufacturer phoned to tell me that on his own he had figured out a love-making method very similar to that of the Tao of Loving many years ago. He said that he and his wife taught it to their only son when he was ten because they both believed that a boy should understand the importance of not accidentally impregnating a woman long before he starts to make love. The man thought all schoolboys should be taught the method.

THE EVIL OF THE DOUBLE STANDARD

Gently but firmly, women must help their lovers understand the evil of the double standard and clear them of any prejudices or misconceptions they may have. In the same way, they should make sure that their sons do not form them.

1. *The double standard about birth control.* The worst double standard is of course the attitude that birth control is solely the woman's responsibility. There are two steps you can take to help your love partner understand how extremely important it is for a man to become *safe*. First, gently tell him the harm caused to women by the various birth-control chemicals and implements. Second, tell him what may happen to women if they have to go through an abortion. I have met many women who were severely affected by having an abortion. Here I shall mention an extreme example:

   Several years ago, on a train not far from Stockholm, I met a thin, exceptionally attractive woman of about twenty-five. As we were talking, I noticed a deep scar on her wrist. I had seen such scars before and I knew at once that she had tried to do away with herself. I asked her and she admitted to the fact; she did not say that she had had an abortion. What she did say was that she had had a child and it died. As a result, she tried to kill herself.

   The next day, I phoned a number she gave me. Her mother answered and said that she was still asleep, so the mother and I had a conversation. The mother revealed that the daughter hadn't given birth to a child; it had been aborted, under the strong urging of both her parents. The reason was that the young woman was very gifted and the parents wanted her to become a surgeon.

   Unfortunately, the woman was unable to forget the unborn child. She felt that she had been an accomplice to a murder! She started drinking heavily and attempted suicide twice. Now, more than ten years after the abortion, she is still in a mental institution. She

telephoned me twice, but all she said was: "I'm so sorry! I have dialed a wrong number." I recognized not only her voice but also her peculiar hesitant manner. Both times she stayed on the line for quite a while, but no matter how much I implored her, she refused to speak. She was so afraid!

2. *The double standard against women's initiative.* Currently the media are advising women to take a stronger initiative in love affairs. I am all for that; in fact, I enjoy it immensely whenever a woman takes the initiative. But a note of caution here: It must be done tactfully. When initiative is combined with the Tao, it usually will succeed. Without the Tao, the woman must be very careful not to make a man feel afraid. The following story illustrates what I mean:

Maija is twenty-six, with a beautiful face and a superb figure. She is extremely reticent in expressing affection, for she learned an unhappy lesson two years ago. At the time, she was living with her husband, Tom. He was a very handsome man but diffident as a lover. And that was due at least in part to his habit of masturbating almost daily since his early childhood. Furthermore, he had always masturbated with a sense of fear and shame.

After two years of marriage, Tom still masturbated almost daily, in secret; of course Maija eventually discovered this. Though she was not pleased with the discovery, it would not have bothered her much if Tom had made love to her often enough to please her. That was not the case. And living with a man but with so little love-making was more than Maija could stand. She decided to take steps to change the situation.

One evening after dinner Maija took the initiative for the first time and tried to coax Tom into making love. It was like an explosion. Tom became insanely furious and told her never to do that again and always to wait for him to take the first step. What Maija did not know was that an insecure lover is constantly in fear of being detected and hates to have his inability to love exposed. The outburst so shocked Maija that she subsequently became one of the most silent women I have ever known. She told me herself that she had not been so reticent before the episode.

3. *The double standard against the single mother.* Many men today still display too little respect for women. Divorcees and single mothers, for example, are regarded as "easy" women. Rut has lived as a lonely mother with her two children for the past six years. She is devoted to her five-year-old son and seven-year-old daughter, but being a healthy woman, she naturally needs the company of men. And being a very attractive woman, she has no problem meeting them. Then what does she complain about?

Rut's voluptuous body triggers many men's lusty imaginations when they meet her, and she is as a rule very responsive when she finds a man pleasing. Before she lets a man make love to her, invariably he is charm itself. Afterward, however, his whole attitude changes. Far from being affectionate, he becomes cold and indifferent. He usually will not even give her his telephone number before leaving. At most he will say only that he will phone sometime. Still, he is not quite as despicable as the men described by Germaine Greer in her book *The Female Eunuch:*

> In the moment immediately after ejaculation they felt murderously disgusted. "For when I'm finished I'm finished. I wanted to strangle her right there in my bed and then go to sleep." . . . *

Even the most affectionate of men often become indifferent after an ejaculation—and for this the only true remedy is learning the Tao. A man should learn to be more respectful and throw away the dreadful double standard. Otherwise, women will become more and more suspicious of men and less and less willing to be approached by them.

4. *The double standard against plain women.* Hanna's story illustrates one more double standard against women. Hanna works in an office in Stockholm. She is blond but not beautiful by Swedish standards. Still, she is healthy and sexy, and she needs a man. Like their counterparts throughout the world, Swedish men are often snobbish in seeking a mate. They prefer to have women whom they can show off instead of women with whom they can live in harmony.

*Germaine Greer, *The Female Eunuch* (London: MacGibbon & Kee, 1970), p. 249.

Hanna travels to the south of Europe whenever she can save enough money for the journey. In the south she becomes popular and sought after just because she is a blonde, a rarity there. Naturally she is very proud of that fact and is very frank in discussing her adventures. Thus her stories have become well known throughout the office. Nearly all her colleagues, especially the men, call her "Shit Hanna" behind her back, some even to her face.

Hanna protests vigorously to those men who tease her: "You are all such hypocrites. Many of you do exactly the same thing as I do when you travel. Just because I am a woman, you give me a name. What should I do? Obviously I do like and need men. But no one loves me here. So why shouldn't I go where I can find people who do?"

Of course, if these men had learned the Tao, they would not be so hypocritical. And Hanna would not have to make such long journeys to find men. For men would then have much more energy to spare and would understand that a beautiful face is not an important factor in loving harmony between Yin (female) and Yang (male). They would also realize that every woman, no matter how old or how plain, has the right to love and sex.

5. *The double standard against sexy women.* There are two unjust and arbitrary terms used to describe a woman's sexual inclinations. A very sexy girl or woman is often called a *nymphomaniac,* especially if she likes to experiment with various types of men. And she is usually regarded as mentally sick. A man of similar tendency is often called a *stud.* He is far from being regarded as mentally ill. The term is even looked upon as a praise or honor, and for that he can feel very proud of himself.

If a woman is passive and is not fond of love-making, she is branded with the term *frigid.* She is also considered mentally abnormal and in need of psychiatric care. If this behavior were indeed a mental abnormality, then a very large number of women would need professional help. And where would we find the millions of psychiatrists needed for this service—especially if we regard as frigid any woman who is unable to have a spontaneous orgasm when making love even when she enjoys it immensely? David Reuben is one of those who

classify all such women as frigid and in need of professional help.*
Because of its importance, we shall devote the entire next chapter to
the subject of frigidity.

The following is a story of an adolescent girl who was supposed-
ly suffering from the relatively rare "nymphomania": On a train re-
turning from Paris, I met a woman painter who told me about her
neighbor's teenage daughter. The girl had been committed to a mental
institution by her parents for no other reason than that she was fond of
making love with many boys. The artist told me that the girl was
healthy, talented, and affectionate. To put such a person in a mental
hospital is truly a crime against human nature and human rights. It
seemed clear to me that the girl's extreme fondness for love-making
stemmed from her love starvation at home.

Some historical facts on the subject may help women change men's
prejudices and double standards. Most of the original Taoists many
thousands of years ago were in favor of a single standard. Without close
collaboration between the sexes, they couldn't possibly have made the
Tao of Loving as useful as it is.

Nearly all the ancient texts for the Tao of Loving mention Huang Ti
(The Yellow Emperor) and Su Nü (the emperor's chief female adviser on
the Tao). Their dialogues mainly concern the vital importance of the complete harmony of Yin and Yang. Thus Su Nü might be considered the first
heroine (historical or legendary) in favor of a single standard.

The West has a similar heroine. In seventeenth-century France one
woman struggled for many years of her long life to attain sexual equality
for women. Her name was Ninon de Lenclos (1620–1706), and she was
quite successful. The story I am going to tell here is based mainly on two
books: *Correspondence Authentique de Ninon de Lenclos*, by Emile Co-
lombey, published in the nineteenth century; and *Ninon de Lenclos*, by
Emile Magne, published in 1948. Ninon exerted a strong influence on the
French's women's liberation movement during the last thirty years of her
life. She believed everyone, man or woman, should develop individual
qualities without imitating or copying anyone else. Nor should anyone be
a slave of fashion. In order to love freely, she gave up marriage.

*David Reuben, *Everything You Always Wanted to Know About Sex*, pp. 111–139.

Her father was a freethinking man who appears to have formed Ninon's basic character. She had almost no formal education except for her father's early teachings in philosophy, music, and languages. She was mainly self-educated. Famous for her beauty and wit, Ninon conducted a salon in Paris that attracted the most distinguished men of her day, many of whom—including the great Condé, La Rochefoucauld, and Saint-Éveremont—were among her lovers. She believed a woman had the same right to court any man she desired and to take as much initiative in approaching men as men did in seeking women.

Because of her belief in equal rights for women and her own free-loving life, she was disliked and even hated by the religious devouts. In 1656, when she was thirty-six years old, she was imprisoned in a convent. But she was fortunate. The abdicated Queen of Sweden, Christina, was visiting France at the time. The young queen was obviously an early feminist, whose refusal of marriage was the main reason for her abdication at the age of twenty-eight. When she heard of Ninon's imprisonment (Christina was six years younger than Ninon), she went to visit her in jail. Afterward Christina went to see King Louis XIV and asked him to release Ninon. The king did.

After her visit from the former queen and her freedom by king's order, Ninon became an honored person in France. Even the courtiers sent their sons to her salon to profit from her teachings. She was known to teach them to treat women as equals, to behave with good manners toward women, and to learn how to be liked and loved by the women they wished to love. It is not clearly known whether she also made love with her pupils.

The religious devouts accused her of corrupting youth. But her supporters said that she was a good teacher. Chavagnac wrote: "When a courtier had a son growing up, he sent him to Ninon. Her way of teaching was excellent, and people can easily notice the difference in behavior between her pupils and other men. She taught them nice ways of courting women, cultivated ways of talking, and so on. In other words, she made gentlemen out of them."

During the last thirty years of her life, Ninon was so honored that even the king often asked her opinions about social affairs. This seems a fit ending to a life devoted to women's equality and a single standard for both sexes. Without a single standard, there is no true liberation for women.

8. FRIGIDITY, SANITY, AND THE TAO

*I never remember
Any enjoyment of my body.*

VIRGINIA WOOLF

Not long before she drowned herself, Virginia Woolf made the above remark to her doctor. She suffered from so-called frigidity nearly all her adult life.

In the previous chapter I mentioned that frigidity is an unjust and arbitrary term applied to women. It is especially unfair because it is a condition artificially and forcibly created by men. What I mean is that for many thousands of years men have subjugated women by brute force and then continually kept them down, in second-class status or even in semi-slavery, by arbitrary laws and moral codes. During all that time, men have never cared much about whether women enjoyed love-making.

This was especially true during the Puritan period in Europe and North America, and in the Victorian era. In those times women were regarded mainly as mere machines for producing children. And good, moral women were not even supposed to feel any pleasure during love-making. Only in the last fifty years or so have men begun to notice that it is really much more satisfying to have women who are active, feeling love partners. Women themselves have also started to become conscious of their sexuality.

After many hundreds of years of suppression, it is only natural that a large number of women still do not respond well to their partial liberation. And the fact remains that many men still behave like overlords toward women. For example, the largest tribe in Kenya today still practices the atrocious custom of amputating the clitoris of female infants. And not long ago many African immigrants carried out that custom here in Sweden, performed by Swedish doctors. It created a public scandal and was soon forbidden by law.

Virginia Woolf was a prominent victim of our half-liberated society. Because she was a famous writer, and also because she committed suicide at the peak of her career, her life was exceptionally well documented. It is well known that she suffered several nervous breakdowns and was fond of women. Above all, she was "frigid."

According to the Tao, however, her problems were created primarily by men's unsympathetic behavior. For example, her lesbian tendencies might not have been formed, and her breakdown avoided, if she had not been molested by her half-brother Gerald Duckworth when she was only six and he was in his twenties. He stood her on a ledge and explored her genitals with his hand. When she was in her teens, George Duckworth, her other half-brother, often came to her room at night without warning, flinging himself on her bed and fondling her.

These love-starved half-brothers certainly left damaging marks on her psyche when it came to men. No wonder she was frigid! Eventually she did meet a man to her liking—Leonard Woolf, who was certainly her intellectual equal but not at all the right person to arouse her physically. There is strong evidence that he was not particularly fond of love-making: "As he reported to Strachey, he found horse riding in the jungle 'better I think as a pleasure than copulation.' "*

*Jonathan Spater and Ian Parsons, *A Marriage of True Minds* (London: Hogarth, 1977), p. 53.

They were married when she was thirty. Their love-making was disastrous. Soon they stopped trying entirely and lived together for twenty-eight more years without making love. If Leonard had had the knowledge of the Tao, he might have been able to help Virginia out of her psychic ambivalence. Their failure in love-making was a great disappointment to her. In a letter to Roger Fry dated May 18, 1923, she said: "But at my time of life, I began to resent inhibition to intercourse. . . ."* In this remark she pinpoints the ailment, and the frigidity, not only of women but of our society as a whole!

FRIGIDITY AND YIN-YANG HARMONY

When Yin and Yang are in harmony.
All diseases in a woman will vanish.
Her complexion will sparkle,
And she will retain her youth like a child.
Try to know the Tao
And to make love very often accordingly.
Then she will enjoy life so much that
Five days without food she'll not suffer.

FROM *Yü Fan Pi Chü*

Eric Fromm once said that a man's confidence in his performance is essential to adequate male sexual functioning and that a woman's ability to trust is essential to adequate female sexual functioning.†

Taboos and repressive laws are the creations of men who lack confidence. Confident men as a rule are good lovers, and they want their women to be free and responsive. Unfortunately, such men are rare. By the time you have finished reading this chapter you'll understand why so many men behave like bullies toward women, treat them abominably by violating their basic human rights, and then outrageously call them frigid! What do they expect?

---

*Nigel Nicolson, ed., *A Change of Perspective* (London: Hogarth, 1977), p. 38.
†Quoted in E.G. Witenberg, ed., *Interpersonal Exploration in Psychoanalysis* (New York: Basic Books, 1973), pp. 189–190.

Men must first make themselves lovable. Many rich men know that love cannot be bought, and it certainly can never be forced. Before a woman can love a man wholeheartedly, she has to trust him and like him. Still today many men make women afraid of them. When there is fear there can never be genuine trust or love. Virginia Woolf's half-brothers, for example, frightened her in a way that made it difficult for her to ever truly love men. This deprived both her and her husband of the vitally important harmony of Yin and Yang. They failed to achieve the total union of their bodies and souls.

Why do most men behave so repressively toward women? Why do they make themselves unlikable or even feared? The fundamental reason for their aggressiveness is that sexually they are much weaker than women in general. They are afraid of women, especially in love-making. The cultured and intelligent artist Edward Munch was deeply afraid of women. He painted many paintings entitled *Vampire* on the theme of a young woman kissing a young man's neck like a vampire sucking off someone's blood. Munch never dared to be intimate with women. But he did appreciate feminine beauty. It must have been hell for him to be so near his models, looking at the beautiful forms of their bodies, without touching them. Perhaps he was afraid that they might kill him, for he strongly believed that his brother Andreas, who died only six months after his marriage, was virtually killed by making love too much with his young, beautiful, and energetic wife.

Can too much love-making kill a man? The ancient Chinese believed that it could if a man made love in the ordinary way; that is why the ancient Taoists formulated a different way of love-making and called it the Tao of Loving. In the Tao's way, love-making can only be beneficial to both sexes, and the more love-making the better.

THE VULNERABLE MALE SEX

But man is only briefly competent;
And only then in the moderate measure applicable to the word in his
*   sex's case.*
He is competent from the age of sixteen or seventeen thenceforward for
*   thirty-five years.*

After fifty his performance is of poor quality;
The intervals between are wide,
And its satisfaction of no great value to either party;
Whereas his grandmother is as good as new.
There is nothing the matter with her plant.
Her candlestick is as firm as ever,
Whereas his candle is increasingly softened and weakened by the
*   weather of age,*
As the years go by, until at last it can no longer stand,
And is mournfully laid to rest in the hope of a blessed resurrection
Which is never to come.

His procreative competency is limited to an average of a hundred
*   exercises per year for fifty years.*
Hers is good for 3,000 a year for that whole time—and as many longer as
*   she may live.*
Thus his life interest in the matter is 5,000 refreshments,
While hers is 150,000.
Yet instead of fairly and honorably leaving the making of the law [of
*   monogamy] to the person who has an overwhelming interest at*
*   stake in it,*
This immeasurable hog, who has nothing at stake in it worth
*   considering,*
*Makes it himself!**

More than half a century after Mark Twain wrote these lines, Erica Jong reached a similar conclusion in her *Fear of Flying:*

> The older you got, the clearer it became that men were basically terrified of women. Some secretly, some openly. What could be more poignant than a liberated woman eye to eye with a limp prick? All history's great issues paled by comparison with these two quintessential objects: the eternal woman and the eternal limp prick. . . . That was the basic inequity which could *never be righted:* Not that the male had a wonderful added attraction called a penis, but that the female had a wonderful all-weather cunt. Neither storm nor sleet nor dark of night could faze it. It was always there, always ready. Quite terrifying, when you think about it. No wonder men hated women. No wonder they invented the myth of female inadequacy.†

*Mark Twain, *Letters from the Earth* (New York: Harper & Row, 1962), pp. 40–41. (Put into poetic form by Jolan Chang.)
†Erica Jong, *Fear of Flying* (New York: New American Library, 1974).

81

Men are not really enemies of women, nor are they dangerous. What is dangerous and ought to be corrected is the mutual fear and distrust between the sexes. Men counter women's sexual power effectively with brutal physical force, thus keeping women in second place. Fortunately, many wiser men have realized that a world dominated by fear and force cannot survive. And with the help of the Tao, men no longer have to fear women. Mastering the Tao can make any man the sexual equal of almost any woman, and can invalidate both Mark Twain's and Erica Jong's fears. With the Tao, men and women can become true loving and equal partners, thus making the age-old conflict between the sexes a thing of the past.

FRIGIDITY CAN BE OVERCOME

With the help of the Tao, frigidity can easily be overcome. First, however, we must refrain from calling women frigid when they enjoy love-making but are not orgasmic. All reputable therapists and physicians, including Masters and Johnson* and Helen Singer Kaplan,† agree that orgasm is a very individual, confusing, and controversial subject. I therefore advise women not to take orgasm too seriously. The main thing is to feel pleasure in love-making. Sooner or later the orgasm will come, and then perhaps a woman will even be disappointed because it is not all as wonderful as she expected.

The best definition of frigidity is the condition of those who do not feel the pleasure of love-making. Following are some of the variations.

I. *Frigidity caused by abortion.* Many women suffer a certain degree of frigidity after an abortion. The problem is more prevalent than is generally suspected. Most women will need time to rekindle their interest in love-making, and even after a long period of time, the right partner will be crucial.

---

*Masters and Johnson, *Human Sexual Inadequacy* (New York: Bantam, 1971), p. 242.
†Helen Singer Kaplan, *The New Sex Therapy* (New York: Brunner-Mazel, 1974), pp. 374–381.

A twenty-eight-year old woman named Lisa, for example, suffered a lengthy period of indifference to love-making after an abortion. For over two years after her abortion she was not very interested in making love. Then one Sunday she made love with a man eight times in three hours. Her frigidity was thawed temporarily and she became warm and passionate toward the man. But of course a man of such ability is very rare, unless he has learned the Tao.

2. *Frigidity caused by a repressive man.* Helena, married for nine years to a very dominating man, felt absolutely nothing in making love with her husband. Then she met a man who was gentler and kinder than her husband and suddenly felt a very different experience in making love. Unfortunately, the man was married and the relationship soon terminated. She went on with her joyless marriage for three more years before she divorced her husband.

Two years later she met a man who had read my first book and who had started to practice the Tao. They began to make love regularly. From the very beginning Helena felt warmth and passion toward him. Their love-making became increasingly satisfying, and eventually she became orgasmic. Now each time she has an orgasm she feels immense pleasure, as if walking on air, but she also feels great fatigue. She then has to refrain from love-making for three or four days before she becomes responsive again. Once when she was exceptionally passionate she assumed the female superior position, staying there for about half an hour and experiencing half a dozen orgasms. After that she did not wish to make love for more than two weeks.

3. *Frigidity caused by lack of love-making.* Sexual response is like any other body functioning. If our sexual organs are not used for a long period of time, much activity may be required before they function successfully once again. Try not lifting one of your arms for a month and you'll be quite alarmed at the problems that result. But most people seldom think of sexual functioning that way until the problem arises.

Anna is such a case. She is thirty-seven and university educated, with a secure profession. Until recently, her love life was next to zero.

She has made love to five men in her life and lived with one of them for two years. But that was not at all a happy relationship. The man took advantage of her, financially and otherwise. After that she had sporadic affairs with three other men, and they all seemed to pronounce her frigid (one of the men was even her physician). Eventually she came to believe it herself, because she never felt much pleasure in love-making. She read my first book and then, quite fortunately, met a man who also had read the book. They started to practice the Tao together. Miraculously, in just one week of love-making in the way of the Tao, her frigidity was thawed.

The three types of frigidity described above can all be overcome if the woman and her partner make love in the way of the Tao. The logical solution to the problem is, of course, to disseminate knowledge of the Tao as we discussed in the preceding chapter and for women to take an active part in teaching and influencing our present generation and our future generations.

THE TAO CURES FRIGIDITY AND BRINGS HARMONY
TO BODY AND SOUL

Same mind, same desire.
Two bodies complementing,
Two mouths connecting.
They inhale each other's fragrant breaths
And they drink each other's nectar.
They caress, touch, and kiss everywhere.
A thousand charms appear,
One hundred worries vanish.
She endears his yü-chin,
And he her yü-mên
Thus his Yang is complemented by her Yin
and his yü-chin is stirred and up,
Like a lonely cliff by the sea.
Her Yin is affected by his Yang,

And her coral cave is inundated and overflowing,
Like a silent spring descending a deep valley.

FROM *Tung Hsüan Tzu*
CHAPTER 5

When a woman and a man are as harmonious as in the quotation above, insanity is almost impossible. That is not only the view of the Tao. Most prominent psychiatrists of our century are of a similar view. We need not restrict ourselves to Freud or Reich and their followers. Even the dean of American psychiatrists, Karl Menninger, was of the view that when a person enjoys sufficient love, insanity is not likely to occur. He calls this beneficial effect "erotic neutralization."*

I have known many people whose love hunger has severely affected their mental stability. The following is an example:

After having two daughters, Mona's mother wished openly to have a son. When the third child turned out to be a girl, she resented the fact deeply. Mona, the unfortunate third daughter, was the victim. Even though the mother had a son two years later, she continued to withhold love and affection from her daughter. In addition, Mona's mother brought her up very strictly, warning her about the dangers of men. Though Mona was very attractive in a womanly way, her mother never did anything to boost her daughter's self-confidence.

Mona had her first breakdown when she was twenty-one. She was hospitalized for several months and had a series of shock treatments. She was hospitalized again when she was twenty-three after attempting to take her life by swallowing sleeping pills. This time she refused the shock treatments. She was out of the hospital half a year later. But she continued to have fits of violent screaming, during which she would break furnishings and windows in her flat and bite her hands until they bled. Fortunately, during that period she managed to find a job that she liked.

When she was twenty-five, Mona met a man whom she became very fond of. She was still a virgin then and in the beginning she felt almost no pleasure in their love-making. Occasionally she had fits of

*Karl Menninger, *Man Against Himself* (New York: Harcourt, Brace, 1972).

violence while he was present, and they shocked him a little. However, the man was tender and a competent lover in the way of the Tao. In about two months she began to thaw even to the degree of being passionate. Her fits came less and less often, and in much milder form. Their relationship has gone on for three years and she is now a happy woman no longer tormented by violent seizures.

9. THE TAO'S SECRET OF YOUTH

COMBINING THE BEST OF TWO WORLDS

I think we would all agree that the most advantageous position to be in in life is to combine the health, vigor, and appearance of youth with the learning and experience that comes with age.

To live to an advanced age without being healthy enough to enjoy life or to contribute to it constructively is not the goal, lest we become a burden to society and an object of pity instead of love. This is mere existence, not living.

Over many thousands of years the Tao developed an effective way of maintaining youth so that people could combine the best of both the young and the aged. It is a great pity that for the last four hundred years very few people seem to have taken full advantage of that knowledge.

Today much is being done to boost public health by promoting better eating habits, regular exercise, and so on. But nearly all these programs lack a decisive psychological factor—the incentive for living which the Tao so amply provides. The individual must very much want to make the effort to maintain his or her youth through the years. Otherwise, he or she will lack the necessary will power to carry out the program successfully.

WHAT IS THE TAO'S SECRET INCENTIVE?

People often fail on the verge of success.
By giving as much care to the end as to the beginning,
There will be few failures.

FROM *Tao Te Ching*
CHAPTER 64

In the industrialized nations of the West, musicians and sportsmen generally enjoy relatively healthier and longer lives than most people. There are two simple reasons: Besides being more physically active than people in a great many other professions, both sportsmen and musicians generally share one essential incentive for living—they genuinely enjoy their work. Playing sports or music well gives a total pleasure to both body and mind that is akin to the pleasure of a well-matched love partnership. Also both professions demand top physical condition, another prerequisite for being a good lover, for either sex.

What is the Tao's incentive for living? It is a happy and highly enjoyable love life right to the very end. This does not mean just maintaining sexual functioning. Rather, the Tao can make the love life of the old *even more satisfying than that of the young.*

The body of a man who makes love frequently and in the way prescribed by the Tao can produce almost as much testosterone as a youth. It is a well-known fact that testosterone is an anabolic hormone that will make a man feel much healthier and stronger and look much younger than his age. And nearly any loving stimulation will increase the amount of testosterone in a man's bloodstream. This fact was proven by research carried out in 1974 by Max Planck Institute for Psychiatry in Munich by endocrinologist Karl M. Pirke and his colleagues. According to the Munich research, even visual sexual stimulation can increase a man's hormone level. Then of course ample actual caressing and love-making as the Tao advises will be even more effective.* When we can anticipate such pleasure, why would we wish to cut our lives short? And who would not try his or her best to keep fit and youthful as long as possible?

In this chapter we shall examine the various ways recommended in the Tao for maintaining good health.

YOUR SWEET BREATH (CORRECT BREATHING)

We shall first talk about breathing, not only because of its importance but also because it is the easiest task to perform and because air is the cheapest nutrient we can have.

1. Deep diaphragmatic breathing will exchange the contents of the lungs completely and make the digestive organs function better, thus eliminating two major causes of bad breath.

2. A deep breather is usually a quieter bed partner. Why? Because a deep breather breathes in and out about seven or eight times a minute when sleeping, while a short breather takes twenty breaths or more in the same period. Thus a short breather makes far more noise than a person who takes in air in long, deep, and smooth motions.

3. A deep breather is far less likely to suffer from insomnia. And it is no exaggeration to say that proper breathing plus correct eating and loving habits will virtually eliminate the need for tranquilizers or headache pills! A deep breather is simply much less nervous and is not easily aroused to anger, which is a major cause of sleeplessness.

4. Deep breathers become tired less easily. Deeper and slower breathing requires less energy. First, breathe with your diaphragm, not your shoulders. Pull the air in downward, never upward. Second, learn to fill your lungs completely with air. Most people fill their lungs to less than 20 percent of capacity. To fill them completely, you must make room, which means you should expel as much of the used air as possible. But expel it slowly and smoothly so that your air sacs have a chance to utilize the air fully. Breathe in more swiftly.

*For more detailed information, see *The Tao of Love and Sex*, p. 116.

THE IMPORTANCE OF DRINKING WATER

Water is the second cheapest vital essence, yet most people drink far too little of it. Some fanatic "experts" even regard water as an enemy. They drink almost no water. It is no wonder, then, that kidney ailments have become very common all over the globe.

Water helps to prevent not only kidney diseases, but also heart disease and cancer, because it flushes away surplus table salt, of which most people consume far too much. Water also helps to remedy all kinds of joint diseases, such as arthritis and gout, and other diseases too numerous to mention. And water eliminates bad breath. Suffice it to say that three large glasses of relatively pure water first thing in the morning will eliminate a great deal of trouble for nearly all of us.

Of course, you should be very careful about the kind of water you drink. Keep away from hard or polluted water. There is a very simple way to ensure against these dangers. In China, most people drink boiled water. Not only does boiling kill harmful bacteria and protozoa, it also eliminates most of the harmful inorganic minerals that may form stones in your kidneys and your ureters or harden your arteries and capillaries.

Boiling is not quite as thorough as distilling, but it is much simpler and cheaper. In Stockholm, where water is only slightly hard, boiling for over an hour is a satisfactory method. Boiling for more than an hour will evaporate about half the original contents, but a pressure cooker can easily solve that problem. And after a few boilings you will see for yourself that a considerable amount of inorganic material has accumulated on the inside of the pot or pressure cooker.

I drink almost no alcoholic drinks. On very rare occasions I may sip an exceptionally good wine to savor its flavor. Such occasions occur but once a year.

I am one of the very few native Chinese who has never become very interested in tea drinking. I have nothing much against it, and the pros and cons of tea drinking are about equal. But as a fruit and vegetable eater, which I have been most of my life, I have never had much extra space in my stomach for tea.

When I was young, drinking coffee was a novelty in China. I developed a liking for its flavor and enjoyed a cup occasionally. But once when I was at the University of Toronto in Canada, at the International

Students' Club, I drank two cups of coffee at about 2:00 P.M. and felt their effect until 2:00 or 3:00 in the morning. So now I take only a sip now and then.

What else do I drink? As I said before, a fruit and vegetable eater usually does not have much room in his stomach for any kind of liquid. And I drink my three large glasses of cooled boiled water about half an hour to one hour before breakfast. During the day I sometimes drink a little honey water. A healthy and long-living Roman senator, asked by Caesar to reveal the secret of his longevity and strength, reputedly gave this terse answer: "Honey within, oil without."

Before I left China, of course, I drank a great deal of soya milk. It was impossible for me to continue that drink after leaving China, since making tasty soya milk requires special skills and instruments. Sometimes I add soya powder to my regular morning porridge, but with my meals I drink mainly warm skim milk mixed from powder. I do not say that it is the ideal drink. But I have not yet discovered a better alternative. I need milk's protein to balance the vegetable proteins I consume, and I need its high calcium content to balance the high phosphorus content of the wheat germ I consume. Also, milk produced in places like Sweden is usually quite rich in iodine (the cows are regularly fed with it). The iodine compensates for the fact that I use almost no salt (the most common source of most people's iodine).

I drink a quart or more of skim milk daily, but I am not advising all readers to do the same. You have to find out for yourself what amount of milk is best for you. However, if you are not allergic to it, I recommend drinking at least half a quart daily. And skim milk powder is one of the most economical foods you can buy. *Yü Fan Pi Chü*, a seventh-century book of the Tao, states that milk is good for general health. And I am quite certain that it contributes to my good skin condition.

BATHING AND WASHING

During World War II, I had to use cold water all year round for washing. Under those circumstances a little soap is necessary to keep clean. But when ample warm water is available, soap is almost superfluous. Our ancestors lived for thousands of years without such a thing as soap. What irks me is not the cost of soap, but the harm it does to our skin and to our

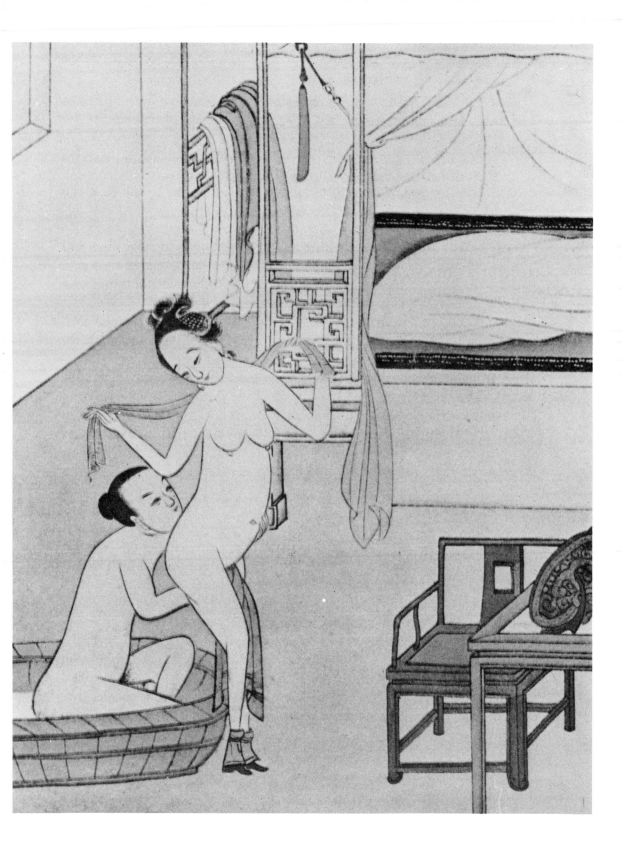

rivers and lakes. Because of its importance, I shall repeat here a piece of scientific information mentioned in an earlier chapter of this book:

> It has been known for some years that unsaturated fatty acids (the main ingredient of most vegetable oils) are an important component of sebum collected from the skin surface, and that they inhibit the growth of several bacterial and fungal cutaneous pathogens.*

Nearly all soaps are alkaline and will neutralize the skin's natural protective fatty acids. Today people use too much soap—and not only on their skin. They overuse nearly all forms of laundry powder or liquid, and through the drains they pollute our lakes and streams.

When I was in my early teens and did not know better, I used soap regularly, and my skin was in a markedly weaker condition in resisting infections than it is today. Now I use almost no soap for my daily bathing except when I come in contact with, say, grease. I have discovered that I can keep myself very clean by a daily warm bath or shower without soap. And I have not had a skin infection for years. Even though most shampoos are neutral in their pH value, I have kept my shoulder-length hair clean and healthy for the last twenty years without using shampoo. I simply wash it vigorously every day with warm jets from the shower.

I have also found a way of washing my bedding and clothing that is ecologically sound. I use laundry powder only when my clothes and linens are visibly stained and need the assistance of a detergent. Normally I just put all sheets, towels, and underwear into a large pot, add hot water, put it on a stove, and boil it. Then I rinse everything out and hang it up. Not only does this method sterilize nearly everything, it also takes out a surprising amount of dirt. This was the way grandmother did laundry before such things as detergent and soap became popular.

The boiling method is ideal for a single, self-employed person. I usually boil my sheets at the same time that I am eating and cooking, so that I can keep an eye on the pot to prevent burning. It has saved me a great deal of time, and I use only a tiny fraction of the laundry powder that most people use. Moreoever, I do not need a machine or visits to a laundromat.

*Mary J. Marples, "Life on the Human Skin," *Scientific American*, January 1969.

VITAMINS AND MINERALS

If you live in a place like Barcelona where fresh fruits and vegetables are abundant and still relatively cheap, you will probably need very little vitamin powder or tablets as a supplement. If you live in Paris, London, or Hamburg you will need more of them. In Stockholm, where I live now, it is almost impossible to maintain optimal health without taking at least one or two grams of vitamin C powder daily.

My mother and I discovered the importance of vitamin C about forty-five years ago, long before Linus Pauling's book *Vitamin C and the Common Cold.* We experimented with oranges and tomatoes and found that we kept ourselves much healthier by eating large quantities of them; even wounds healed much faster. In those days the term *vitamin* was rarely used, but ancient Chinese texts were quite familiar with the beneficial effects of oranges on human health.

Linus Pauling was severely attacked by scientists and physicians following the publication of his book on vitamin C. Now, however, more and more doctors believe that for many people vitamin C is quite effective in preventing colds.

In any case, after reading the University of Dublin's study of vitamin C,* I have been free from colds for the last seven years. The Dublin research very simply indicates that when a man notices signs of a cold, he should take 2.5 grams of vitamin C every six hours until all symptoms disappear. For a woman, the recommended dosage is 2 grams every six hours.

Though I am five feet, nine inches tall, I weigh only 128 pounds, because I am rather small-boned. So whenever I sense a cold coming on, I take 2 grams instead of 2.5 grams. And one or two doses along with a good night's sleep are usually sufficient to shake off the onset of a cold. During the last two years I have succeeded in preventing colds completely by taking half a gram of vitamin C after every main meal, about 2 grams daily in the winter and about 1 gram daily in other seasons. During my first few winters in Sweden, I caught a nasty Stockholm cold in each which would usually take me several weeks to shake off. (I believe it was one of these stubborn Stockholm colds that killed the French philosopher Descartes in

---

*Stephen Rosen, *Future Facts* (New York: Simon & Schuster, 1970), pp. 53–55.

1650, shortly after he came here as Queen Christina's guest and teacher.)

In my experience, vitamin C is not quite as effective if the body lacks vitamins A and D and calcium. And calcium may not be properly absorbed unless we have magnesium from green vegetables. Since I was about fifteen I have been careful to keep my body supplied with vitamins A and D. This may at least partly explain why I am the only member of my family who has perfect eyesight, even though I am over sixty years of age.

THE SUN

The ancient Taoists did not believe in sunbathing. And modern dermatologists fully agree, because too much exposure to the sun's rays can cause skin cancer. Yet the ancient Taoists believed in judicious exposure of the eyes to the sun. They thought that the sun's rays helped promote good eyesight as well as general good health. This theory has recently been supported by American zoologists. For many years zoos in the United States had problems keeping their animals healthy and fertile. But as soon as they started to use sun lamps instead of ordinary lamps to light the interior of the zoos, the situation changed dramatically. The reason is that the sun's rays stimulate the pituitary gland through the eyes; the gland then releases several hormones which are essential to good health and physical well-being.

When sunlight is filtered by glasses or lenses, it will usually lose its beneficial effects. Thus I am sorry to see so many people wearing sunglasses unnecessarily, since they are depriving themselves of the sun's benefit. People who wear contact lenses and corrective glasses are also deprived of this benefit. It is easy enough to remove ordinary glasses and thus to benefit from the sun's rays from time to time, but it is difficult to remove contact lenses every time one goes out in the sun.

Ever since I was a young boy and read about the beneficial effects of the sun in old books, I have sought out the sun's rays. I face the sun and blink my eyes for about a minute whenever sunlight is available.

EXERCISE

> One can take a trip to paradise and stay there to enjoy life for thirty minutes without spending a cent. So it is most advisable for us to adopt T'ai Chi.
>
> MASTER T. T. LIANG
> *T'ai Chi Ch'uan*

In my first book I talked about T'ai Chi Ch'uan, an ideal exercise based on the Tao's idea that perpetual flowing movement keeps water fresh. It is also a most peaceful defense method, for it disarms and wards off an attacker with his own attacking momentum. For details, see Chapter II of my first book.

To conclude this chapter we shall introduce the original Tao's useful concept of perpetual motion, as described in Sun Ssû-Mo's *Priceless Recipe:*

> The Tao for cultivating life is that one must keep oneself as fluid as possible. One should not stand still for too long but neither should one exhaust or force oneself to perform impossible tasks. One should learn by observing that flowing water never putrefies and a busy door does not foster worms, for they exercise and move almost perpetually. . . .
>
> One should not sit or lie in one posture or position for too long. One should put clothes on before one feels too cold and loosen or take them off before one feels too hot. One should eat before one feels too hungry.

People who adopt Master Sun's teaching thoroughly are actually exercising perpetually without especially *doing* it.

A couple of years ago Sweden had a rare strike that kept public transportation at a standstill for about two weeks. As a result, the stores sold out their supplies of bicycles. When the strike was over many of the new cyclists who had discovered the joy and well-being of moving their own legs to go places decided to continue. The result was much like that described in an article in *Cosmopolitan*'s May 1980 London issue: "The 20th Century's Love Affair with the Car Is Waning and in Its Place Comes

Pedalophilia." Cycling is obviously a happy by-product of the oil crisis, for it is one of the few ideal exercises which provides perpetual movement without too much stress. At the same time it is useful and economical, and in crowded cities, it will get you to your destination more quickly than driving.

10. LOVE AND OVEREATING

THE IMPORTANCE OF FINDING A SUITABLE WAY OF EATING

Before my seventeenth year, I was like most people I know, enjoying a love affair with food. I often had the problem of being unable to stop eating, particularly when tempted by the best of China's famous cuisine. When I was fourteen I ate a whole duck and numerous other dishes at a New Year's Eve dinner. And when I was sixteen, after a day's mountain climbing, I ate a tableful of food. What an astonishing waste! I did not become fat, but I often had an upset stomach. Once I began to enjoy love-making, the problem ceased.

In some ways, eating correctly and wholesomely is even more complicated than loving. Loving involves yourself and your love partner, but eating involves hundreds of items about which you have very little knowledge and over which you have even less control.

MY SIMPLE WAY OF EATING

I learned my way of eating mainly from the teachings of Taoist Sun Ssû-Mo, the king of traditional Chinese medicine. He lived for 101 years (A.D. 581–682), and I have repeatedly mentioned him in my first book and in the present volume. His long and healthy life certainly gives weight to his teaching. The following is a summary of what Sun Ssû-Mo said about eating:

1. Rich eating usually cuts life short. Today of course this fact is common knowledge, but 1,300 years ago it was revolutionary news. Sun Ssû-Mo was perhaps the first physician who clearly saw the connection between long life and spare eating.

2. Like nearly all other Tao masters, Sun teaches that loving correctly is of supreme importance. Otherwise, no matter what one eats, one still cannot achieve the ultimate goal of a healthy, long life.

3. Nearly all diseases can be remedied by correcting faulty eating habits. A good physician should always first prescribe better food; medication is in order when the new way of eating has failed to produce results. Major surgery should never be performed except to save a life.

CERTAIN FOODS CAN CURE DISEASE

Tang Emperor Ming-Huang's favorite woman, Yang Kue-Fi, suffered from bad breath. The royal physician prescribed fresh lichee fruit, which grows only in the warm climate of southern parts of China. The imperial capital of Chang-An was a thousand miles away from the northern and southern borders. So the emperor ordered relay horses to transport the precious fruit so his favorite's bad breath could be cured.

This story should correct the incorrect information disseminated by some writers of macrobiotics, who state that people should be careful about foods grown in faraway places that have a very different climate. This is certainly not the traditional macrobiotics of the Tao. Ginseng, for example, a product of the very cold climate of the mountains of China and Korea, has been a favorite health drink of people throughout China for several thousand years. Indeed, it has now become quite popular with people all over the world. Lichee fruit is also popular with the Chinese

everywhere, regardless of climate, and it is of course transported by faster means than the emperor's relay horses.

For some years I was afflicted with clusters of flat warts on my face and forearms. They were unsightly but did not cause any discomfort, and no physician seemed to be able to help me get rid of them. Then one summer I traveled to south China's Guanxi province. Stopping over for several days in a large city called Liuzhou, I discovered a tasty small yellow fruit that grew in clusters like grapes, yet it was different from grapes in that it came from large trees. It was cheap and delicious. For days I must have eaten a very large quantity of the fruit. Then near the end of my stay an interesting thing happened. All the flat warts turned red and fell off, leaving no trace on my face or body. This happened about forty years ago, and I cannot remember the name of the fruit. It is not well known, and I have not seen it anywhere else except in that city. It could be that this small yellow fruit contains a large quantity of the mineral zinc, which is known to be a miraculous cure for certain skin afflictions.

WHAT I EAT AND HOW I EAT

Lawrence Durrell has mentioned in *A Smile in the Mind's Eye* that I eat five or six times daily, consuming food that is large in bulk but low in calories. And I maintain an almost constant body weight of 128 pounds. At a height of five feet, nine inches, this is quite slim. But with my small bones, I feel it is my ideal weight, and I have no difficulty at all maintaining it.

The foods of large bulk that I eat are mainly vegetables and fruits. If my diet includes a large proportion of vegetables, along with a fair amount of fruit, I usually maintain optimal good health. This contradicts some macrobiotic writers' emphasis on cooked whole cereal grains. My view is that most people today consume too much cereal, which contributes to the general overweight of our population. And being overweight is truly one of the great tragedies of our time. It not only wastes energy; it also wears out our bodies in their effort to carry the extra weight.

The true macrobiotic way of eating is flexible, and everyone must find his or her ideal diet by experimenting. For example, I am not a strict vegetarian. I have not eaten meat and poultry for quite some time simply because most animals today are regularly dosed with antibiotics or even with artificial estrogens. In the United States alone in 1978, 8 million pounds of various types of antibiotics were used by farmers, and I can well understand their reason. Animals grow much faster on less feed that way and are less susceptible to disease. The problem with using such drugs is that they greatly increase the antibiotic-resistant strains of bacteria in our bodies. Feeding animals and poultry with artificial estrogens has an equally sinister effect.

I do eat fish frequently, especially fish from the ocean, since oceanic water is not yet badly polluted. My favorite Swedish fish is a flat fish that resembles Dover sole. It comes from the west coast of Sweden and is called red tongue. To prepare something similar, first buy a fresh fish of fairly large size (about one to one and a half pounds). Clean it as usual, but do not remove the skin, head, or bones. Cut it into three pieces (a large center piece and two smaller pieces consisting of the head and tail fin) so that a large frying pan will be able to accommodate the whole fish. Place a layer of vegetables that have been cut into small pieces on the bottom of the pan. This will prevent the fish from sticking to the pan while cooking and will eliminate the need to add oil or fat (most fish have a fair amount of fat, and there is no need to add any).

Put more small pieces of vegetables, along with a few pieces of apple, on top of the fish. Next, add a small piece of ginger that has been cut into minute pieces. Then add a little water so that the dish will not burn. On top of that sprinkle some soya sauce and one or two spoons of cider vinegar. Cover the pan and cook for about ten minutes. You will have a delicious fish dinner for about four people. If you are alone, you can put the pan into the fridge after eating; the fish will last for several days. Serving in the original cooking pot is common in many parts of China, for it saves on dishes.

SOYA BEAN, THE CHINESE COW

Soya bean is perhaps the most economical and nutritious food in the world today. For thousands of years it has been called the Chinese cow. Almost every day in China I ate soya products, including soya milk and soya bean cake (tofu). Tofu is now obtainable in many large Western cities but the price is rather high—except in cities like New York, London, and Toronto, which have large Chinese populations.

One of the simplest ways of cooking soya beans requires a fairly large cooking pot, preferably of stainless steel or enameled steel. Measure out about three cups of soya beans and rinse them over running tap water. Add six to seven cups of cooled boiled water and soak the beans for six to eight hours. Cover the pot, put it on the lowest possible heat on your cooking range, and leave it to simmer for three to four hours. It will then be ready to eat and will last for at least half a week. Be sure to put the pot back in the fridge after each meal (I eat a few spoonfuls of it at every meal).

Experimentation is the best way to become an interesting cook. Many of the directions above are flexible, so that you will be encouraged to experiment. You must find perfection for yourself by trial and error.

Also, I do not know the type of stove or pot you are using, nor do I know your tastes and preferences. For example, when I say you should cook the beans for three to four hours, the time variation allows for your own taste in food. Cooking for four hours will yield much tenderer beans than cooking for three hours. You can, if you wish, cook the beans even longer. Similarly, if you use six cups of water, the results will be drier than if you use seven cups of water. Each variety has its own special flavor. The drier form may taste like roasted chestnuts, and the wetter variety may taste like cooked lotus nuts.

You might try adding some honey when you are eating or serving the beans. You can eat them either warm or cold, to suit your own taste. You can also eat them with bread or rice or with any kind of vegetables. A small portion of cooked soya beans, a few spoons of rice, and some green vegetable leaves cut into small pieces make a truly nutritious, delicious, and economical meal.

SOME OTHER ECONOMICAL YET NUTRITIOUS ITEMS

When I was a young man in China, I ate a lot of eggs. Even today I still eat an occasional egg, which I neither boil nor fry nor scramble. I just crack the egg and leave it on the vegetable pot to be steamed for about one minute (steaming is a very important technique in Chinese cooking). I eat few eggs these days mainly because of the doubtful feed that chickens are getting.

One of the most important food items I now eat daily is wheat germ. It is cheap and is just about the only natural food that has all the known B vitamins and maybe even a few additional ones that have not yet been discovered. It also has vitamin E, the complete and best of proteins, and the highest grade of vegetable oil. I cannot think of another natural food (except perhaps rice polish) that is more complete than ordinary, inexpensive wheat germ.

I mix a few spoonfuls of it with powdered skim milk at almost every meal. I am not particularly partial to the taste of powdered skim milk, but it is certainly very economical and convenient. I must admit that wheat germ tastes much better with buttermilk or yogurt or any other kind of sour milk.

OUR DANGEROUSLY PROLONGED LOVE AFFAIR WITH SWEETS

An overwhelming majority of people the world over are digging early graves with their teeth and tongues. When we were children, before we had our first love partner, we could not control our desire for sweets. With all the varieties of ice cream, candies, chocolates, and cakes available to us as children, we did not have much of a chance of winning the war against overeating. But once we learn to enjoy the truly heavenly joy of lovemaking, we should have a much better chance.

The only true cure for our dangerous love affair with overeating is to find something—someone—else to love: to love completely, mentally and physically.

11. THE TAO IN A NUTSHELL

To put the Tao in a nutshell: "Stop destroying and stop creating problems for others and yourself! Start to enjoy and appreciate love, beauty, and life."

Some time ago I received an interesting letter from the popular Danish writer Suzanne Brøgger. It ended with this incisive remark: "Looking forward to seeing you. Because if I am into any 'ism' at all, it is the Tao—which is *not* an 'ism'!"

THE TAO IS NOT A RELIGION

The best of man is like water.
Water benefits millions of things

Yet does not compete with them.
It dwells in lowly places
That others disdain.
And that is the Tao.

FROM *Tao Te Ching*
CHAPTER 8

In its benevolence, its flexibility, and its lack of formality, water is the symbol of the Tao. Nearly all organized religions, on the other hand, are full of ritual and dogma. Hence, by its nature and essential character, the Tao is not a religion.

In the 2,500 years since the appearance of the *Tao Te Ching*, numerous attempts have been made to make the Tao a religion. It is somewhat like the deification of Gandhi by his followers after his death. How ironic that many have made a god of a man who was perhaps the most humble and least lordly public figure of our century. Fortunately, the deification of the Tao has not been very successful. It remains primarily a philosophy. (Even though there were a few Taoist temples in China when I was there many years ago, the number of Buddhist temples was at least ten times greater.)

THE TAO IS NOT ANARCHISM

The best of man is pragmatic and down to earth
In thinking he is profound
In relations with others he is kind and friendly
In words he is sincere and keeps promises
In government he works for harmony and peace
In affairs he selects the ablest
In action he chooses the best of timing.

FROM *Tao Te Ching*
CHAPTER 8

Shortly before Mao Zedong died, I was on a train leaving Vienna for Paris, sharing a compartment with an Austrian ecologist from the UN. During our conversation he said: "You may not believe that only a few days ago I was in Peking and had lunch with Fung Yu-Lun. And Fung told me that he was writing probably his last book, a book about Mao Zedong as a Taoist."

In my first book I pointed out an old saying: "If Confucianism is the outer garment of the Chinese, Taoism is its soul." Mao called himself a Communist; others call him the founder of Maoism. Still, at heart he can be considered a Taoist. And he certainly learned well the advice of the *Tao Te Ching* quoted above. No matter what people may think of him, he certainly formed the most effective Chinese government in the last two hundred years. And that is, of course, not anarchism.

Mao's reputation has been tarnished since the Cultural Revolution. And the cruel behavior of his wife also did some damage. But many still regard him as an outstanding personality, and he had an undeniably profound effect in bringing modern China together.

As a political leader and strategist, Mao was a superb student of the Tao. I would not, however, call him a complete Taoist, for he had only scant knowledge of the vitally important Tao of Loving, which makes the Tao an unique philosophy. (Without the Tao of Loving, the Tao would become mostly just empty talk. Indeed, the seventh-century giant in medicine, Sun Ssû-Mo, considered it so important that he often simply called the Tao of Loving the Tao.*)

If Mao had understood the vital importance of the Tao of Loving, China would not have gone through a puritanical period after the revolution and he himself would have enjoyed much better health, instead of indulging in food and cigarettes during his later years.

Mao's relative ignorance of the Tao of Loving is not really extraordinary, for very few Chinese scholars of his generation had a comprehensive understanding of it. Those who did remained silent, owing to the puritanical atmosphere in China after the 1949 revolution. Still, Mao was perhaps the most humanitarian revolutionary of our century. The following is a rather reliable story:

For many years Mao had a principal rival for party leadership in the person of Chang Ko-Tau. In the end Mao won and Chang fled to Hong Kong. One day after Mao had succeeded in unifying China, he invited Chang's wife (who had remained behind with her family) to visit him. Mao said to her: "I have heard that your husband is sick in Hong Kong. I think you and the family should join him there and look after him." Mao

*For more information about Sun Ssû-Mo, see *The Tao of Love and Sex*, pp. 53–55, 114–115, 117–120.

sent the family to Hong Kong with sufficient funds for Chang Ko-Tau's old age.

I heard this story from a family friend of Chang Ko-Tau. What a dramatic contrast it is to most stories of political rivalry, especially in countries that have had revolutions in our century.

Even though China today is not quite as puritanical as it was some years ago (especially during the Cultural Revolution), there is still no popular information about the Tao of Loving. A Chinese engineer who has lived and worked here in Sweden for over twenty years visited China last year. When he came back he telephoned me to ask whether my first book was available in Chinese. He was very disappointed when I said no because he thought his brother in China needed my book desperately.

LOVE IS THE BACKBONE

The Tao has three treasures.
Hold and keep them always:
The first is universal love.
The next is not to be wasteful.
The third is humility.

FROM *Tao Te Ching*
CHAPTER 67

To love, it is necessary to be loved. There are many mothers who cannot truly love their children because they themselves are not loved. Remember that one may say "I love you, I love you!" a thousand times, but it is still just an empty sound to a lover or a child. They expect a love of substance, of loving actions and caresses.

I cannot help but notice that my boy's mother transforms into a truly angelic woman when she is fully satisfied and happy. And for that you may be surprised to learn that she needs much love-making. Often she wants to go on and on! And that is beyond the ability of a man who has not learned the Tao of Loving.

The *Tao Te Ching* describes the first treasure of the Tao as universal love. (Professor Chan Wing-Tsit translates it a little differently as "deep

love."*) There is nothing much else in the *Tao Te Ching* about love, but underlying the work is a philosophy that regards love as the most important treasure.

But that at least partly explains why the *Tao Te Ching* survived the book burning of the Mongols. Both the Mongols and later the Manchus, foreigners who conquered China for two separate periods, feared the Tao as the true spirit and force of China. Both did a thorough job of smothering the Tao as a philosophy. They did so by taking out its backbone—the Tao of Loving—which almost disappeared during their rule.

A TAOIST IS AN OPTIMIST

We all like to be comfortable and happy. But the overwhelming majority of us have neither comfort nor happiness. Most people erroneously equate their "living standard" and happiness with the amount of money they make and spend. So almost everyone is vying for more and more money in hundreds of ways. All crimes, dishonest deeds, and wars have their root in this greedy struggle for money.

And the certain by-product of this greedy struggle is an enormous waste of human and natural resources. Clever people will continue to contrive new schemes to accumulate money. Some of them make novel and useful commodities. Most of them, however, accumulate money by making useless but enticing products. We can see for ourselves that more than half of what is in the market today has dubious value and usefulness. By manufacturing these products, we waste not only time and energy but also natural resources, which become scarcer every day.

Invariably, the happiest men and women are those who are very much loved by their mates, friends, and acquaintances; the unhappiest ones are always the loneliest. Wealth has little to do with it. So it all comes down to the conclusion of the Tao that the harmony of Yin and Yang is essential to the well-being and happiness of us all.

The struggle for material wealth is no way to happiness. Nearly all

---

*Chan Wing-Tsit, *A Source Book in Chinese Philosophy* (Princeton, N.J.: Princeton University Press, 1969), p. 171.

thinking people have begun to see our perilous way of living. Yet a large number of them would say pessimistically that it is useless to go against the trend of society. The Tao tells us otherwise:

We must cease that hopeless pessimism,
And stop singing that gloomy song of certain death!
For there is a much happier and healthier
Destination of life and love.

12. THE TAO AND THE IDEAL WORLD

An ideal life is to make ourselves and others happy
At the same time harm no one including ourselves,
And then do our best to contribute to our society,
So that it will not only be saved from destruction,
But also become an increasingly more beautiful and loving society.

ANONYMOUS

The late historian Arnold Toynbee said something to the effect that the industrialization of the West would not have been possible without its puritanical restraint. Westerners have diverted their time and energy from sexual pleasure to learning and mastering complicated technology.

Mary Jane Sherfey promulgates a similar theory, but accentuates the immense female sexual drive and widens its scope from the industrialization of the West to the modernization of all human society:

> All relevant data from the 12000 to 8000 B.C. period indicate that precivilized woman enjoyed full sexual freedom and was often totally incapable of controlling her sexual drive. Therefore, I propose that one of the reasons for

the long delay between the earliest development of agriculture (c. 12000 B.C.) and the rise of urban life and the beginning of recorded knowledge (c. 8000–5000 B.C.) was the ungovernable cyclic sexual drive of women. Not until these drives were gradually brought under control by rigidly enforced social codes could family life become the stabilizing and creative crucible from which modern civilized man could emerge.*

THE SACRIFICE OF LOVE

Love hunger and deficiency have made a huge number of us ill with fear and suspicion. And what have we gained by sacrificing love? Some people argue that we now have longer and longer life expectancies. But statistical life expectancy is a rather confusing thing. Average life expectancy has increased dramatically during recent years mainly because we have made childbirth much safer. Remember, too, that we now face the possibility of complete destruction of life on earth. This would not have been the case if we had not overindustrialized ourselves!

I don't believe women have gone wild because of full sexual freedom. It could be that men have been and still are somewhat frightened of women's sexual capacity. But that can easily be corrected by learning the Tao, as we have seen.

LOVING SATISFACTION: A GUARANTEED HUMAN RIGHT

Havelock Ellis was perhaps the first Western scholar to observe the extent of women's sexual desire:

> The maximum of the woman's pleasure not being reached until three-quarters of an hour have passed. . . . It may occasionally happen that a little later the woman again experiences desire, and intercourse begins afresh in the same way. But after that she is satisfied, and there is no recurrence of desire.†

Ellis's observation seems on the low side. In my experience, a woman's

*Quoted in Norman Mailer, *The Prisoner of Sex* (New York: Signet, 1972), pp. 56–57.
†Havelock Ellis, *Studies in the Psychology of Sex*, vol. II, part 3 (New York: Random House, 1942), p. 544.

desire may recur many times. On one Saturday, I observed a woman's desire recurring sixteen times! (Of course not every love-making session lasted for three-quarters of an hour.) After that she was in peace for several days. But that was clearly an extreme case.

What I am trying to convey here is that when a man has mastered the Tao, he is easily the sexual equal of any woman. If knowledge of the Tao is widely disseminated "the ungovernable cyclic sexual desire of women" becomes easily satisfied and there is no longer any need to govern or repress that drive. Women who are completely satisfied in love are the most peaceful, positive, and constructive citizens of the world! Only when that is accomplished—when the greater half of our world's population has been thus transformed—can we see a tangible hope for an ideal world!

THE PRISONER OF SEX LIBERATED

Love is the contact between two skins.

JEAN-PAUL SARTRE

Norman Mailer's *Prisoner of Sex* leaves many readers with a bitter taste of hatred and hostility between the sexes. So much energy wasted, so much love cast away on the ground!

Who is the prisoner? No one need be! Love and sex ought to be our best friends, better even than food, sleep, or intellect. We are all bound to our three meals every day, nearly a third of our existence is sleep, and some of us devote the greatest part of our lifetime to learning. Yet few complain that we are prisoners of food, sleep, or learning!

No one is a prisoner of sex. And the pleasures of love and sex are meant for us. They are our natural bounty. When the war between the sexes is over at last, the resulting peace will spread to all classes, nations, and races. It will be an almost automatic step to the ideal world of which we dream!

BIBLIOGRAPHY: CHINESE TEXTS

Su Nü Ching

Su Nü Fang

Yü Fan Pi Chü

Tung Hsüan Tzu, by Li Tung Hsüan (Sui or Tang period)
> The above four books are the 1914 editions edited by Yeh Te Hui, an eminent scholar from Hunan. The authors of the first three are not known, but their date is certainly pre-Tang, probably Han.

Priceless Recipe, by Sun S'sü-Mo (Tang), 1955 reprint of northern Sung Dynasty edition.

Chi Chi Chen Ching, by Lu Tung Pin (Tang)

Hsiu Chen Yen I, by Wu Hsien (Han)

Su Nü Miao Lun, Anonymous
> The above four books were reprinted by van Gulik. Only fifty copies of these works are available, distributed among the major libraries of the world.

Pen Ts'ao Kang Mu, by Li Shih Chen (Ming)

I Hsin Fang, compiled and edited by Tamba Yasuyori, a famous Japanese physician of Chinese descent in A.D. 984. The work consists of extracts from several hundred Chinese books of the Tang period and earlier. Here I have used the 1955 Chinese edition.

Han Wei Ts'ung Shu: ninety-six works by various authors such as the famous poet T'ao Ch'ien and the Taoist Ko Hung of the Chin period (A.D. 265–420).

Shih Chi (Historical Record), by Ssuma Ch'ien (Han)

Ch'ien Han Shu, by Pau Ku (Han)

Hou Han Shu, by Fan Yeh (Lui Sung period, A.D. 450)

Tao Te Ching, by Li Erh (Chou)

Jou Pu Tuan, by Li Yu (Ming)

Hsi Hsiang Chi, by Wang Shin Fu (Yuan)

Chuang-Tzu, by Chung Chou (Chou)

T'ien Ti Yin Yang Chiao Huen Ta Lo Fu, by Po Shin-Chien (Tang)

Shu Chin Yu Lu, by Wu Hsien

Yü Fang Chi Tao, by Pêng Tsu, a seventh-century book of the Tao

INDEX

ABOUT THE AUTHOR

Jolan Chang is the author of the immensely successful *The Tao of Love and Sex* and the subject of Lawrence Durrell's *A Smile in the Mind's Eye*. He lives in Stockholm, Sweden.